NO MORE HEROES

NO MORE HEROES

Dave Hopwood

MILTON KEYNES ● COLORADO SPRINGS ● HYDERABAD

Copyright © 2009 Dave Hopwood

15 14 13 12 11 10 09   8 7 6 5 4 3 2 1

First published 2009 by Authentic Media
9 Holdom Avenue, Bletchley, Milton Keynes, MK1 1QR, UK
1820 Jet Stream Drive, Colorado Springs, CO 80921, USA
Medchal Road, Jeedimetla Village, Secunderabad 500 055, A.P., India
www.authenticmedia.co.uk

Authentic Media is a division of IBS-STL U.K., limited by guarantee, with
its Registered Office at Kingstown Broadway, Carlisle, Cumbria CA3 0HA.
Registered in England & Wales No. 1216232. Registered charity 270162

The right of Dave Hopwood to be identified as the Author of this work has
been asserted by him in accordance with
Copyright, Designs and Patents Act 1988

All rights reserved. No part of this publication may be reproduced, stored in
a retrieval system, or transmitted in any form or by any means, electronic,
mechanical, photocopying, recording or otherwise, without the prior
permission of the publisher or a licence permitting restricted copying. In the
UK such licences are issued by the Copyright Licensing Agency,
90 Tottenham Court Road, London W1P 9HE.

British Library Cataloguing in Publication Data
A catalogue record for this book is available from the British Library

ISBN-13: 978-1-85078-838-6

Cover Design by David Smart
Print Management by Adare
Printed and bound in the UK by J F Print Ltd, Sparkford, Somerset.

For Liz and Martin, for all your friendship, patience and kindness over the years; and for my very good mate Ben, top dude and number one Imagineer, thanks for all your encouragement and for making me a movie star

Contents

Prologue	xi
PART ONE	1
Beginnings	3
The hunt for *Black Hawk Down*	6
The snub	13
Abby	16
Just another concubine	18
Twenty minutes of curiosity	21
Mosher	23
Giants and deserts	27
The victim	28
Mo Mountain	32
The black book	35
The edge of everything	40
About six weeks ago	44
The back of beyond	46
The packet	49
The best movie in the world	52
Running free	56
PART TWO	61
The last man on earth	63
Missing	67
The Memphis	69

The job	71
The next day	75
Brief encounter	78
Dinah	83
Over Eden way	88
Angels in the graveyard	92
Circular rock'n'roll	97
Romeo's baby	100
Disintegrating	106
The key	110
Jake's women	113
Revelations	117
OCD	120
Laban	122
PART THREE	**127**
Haggy	129
Wherever you go	135
Conversion	140
Rhea	144
Anything	147
Normal	154
Wrestling	160
Phil Oakey	163
Raised by wolves	166
Close to home	170
Blood and hate	174
Looking after number one	178
Bitesize anecdotes	185
PART FOUR	**189**
The chase sequence	191
The table	202
Running and hiding	206
The coffee shop	208
The search	212

The battle	218
That cold blast of death	224
Nod's Car Hire	229
The grieving unit	231
Home	232
The favour	237
PART FIVE	243
The Good Lover's Sex Guide	245
Final breaths	256

Prologue

A coffee shop somewhere.

Cain gathered the stray grains of sugar into a little mountain on the table and contemplated his options. The door opened and the draught kicked the menus and newspapers across the nearby tables. He seemed distracted. Lost even. He sat low in his seat as each new customer walked in and he checked the window regularly.

He nervously picked at his fingernails with the edge of the menu.

'What can I get you?' The demure waitress smiled and looked down at him, pen at the ready.

'Americano, please.'

'Anything to eat?'

He ordered bacon and waffles with extra syrup. She went and he leant forward again and studied the street through the window. The chase had robbed him of much appetite but he had to keep his energy up. Sugary junk might just do it.

He sat there in a trance for a while. The food came. He ate some. Kept surveying the half-empty room. Then, when the waitress was out the back, he leapt up and went. She returned to find two other guys in the doorway; one with blond hair with crimson tips, the other with a strange two-level cut, long one side, short the other.

'Seen a tall guy – real beanpole? Mohican hair. Bit messed up, looked like he was on the run?'

The waitress eyed the two guys carefully. This was definitely a day for memorable hair.

'Why?' she asked.

'Why not – have you seen him? Did he come in? Someone down the road said . . .'

She nodded. 'But you're not going to beat him up, are you?'

'No!' said the one with long and short hair. 'Believe it or not, we want to ask him about a DVD.'

'Which one?'

'What does it matter which one?'

'Just wondered.'

'Well, it's not *Notting Hill*, all right?'

She forced a droll laugh. 'Ha ha. Not every woman likes Hugh Grant you know. Matt Damon, maybe . . .'

'Look, we're in a hurry right . . .' the one with red and blond spikes said, starting to leave.

'Have you seen *Amélie*?' she asked.

The other one's face lit up. 'Yeah, brilliant. And the next one, *A Very Long Engagement* – though the title gives it away a bit.'

'I love Audrey Tautou,' she said. 'Though what she was doing in *The Da Vinci Code* I'll never know.'

'Excuse me, Mariella Frostrup,' said the blond one. 'Can we just go please? We're in a hurry.'

She shrugged. 'Just chatting,' she said. They went to the door and yanked it open. She asked another question about the DVD. One of them told her. They went. The last she saw of them they were hurtling down the street.

PART ONE

Beginnings

There was blood everywhere. I mean everywhere. The caesarean had been a hasty job: the twins were at 39 weeks and leaving it much longer would have been dangerous. The mother's eyes were wide with a strange brew of terror and wonder. The wide-eyed stare softened as the surgeon presented her with an instant family. Two blinking, gulping creatures coated in a grey and red slime. Strange ugly aliens that were to her the most beautiful creatures on the planet. The nurse began to wipe them down.

'Never seen that before,' she said. 'The smaller one won't let go of his brother.'

Rebekah looked at the two through tear-drenched eyes. One of the boys was indeed clutching the foot of the other one as if he'd never release it. The child squealed as the nurse unclamped the tiny perfect fingers.

'Come on sweet pea, you've got a good grip,' she said. 'You'll be great at opening jars. That and hanging off cliff faces.'

And before she'd even finished he'd clutched at his mother's little finger and was hanging on for dear life.

The day they were born their father visited his bank, withdrew an obscene amount of money and invested it in a clutch of South African diamonds, which he then deposited in an entirely different bank, in a safety deposit box deep in a chilled vault along with other people's secrets and keepsakes. Their father was an astute and successful businessman. Those diamonds would buy the boys a future.

On the same day Adam's first son plopped out onto an old rug in the family home. The baby's mother had always sworn she'd give birth at home. She'd been through plenty; she wouldn't be fazed by the simple production of a screaming child. When the local midwife arrived Adam was sitting on the floor sweating, with a glass of whisky in one hand and a pair of amniotic-fluid-smeared scissors in the other.

David, meanwhile, was celebrating his boy's second birthday. Champagne flowed and the nightclub was packed with the bodies of the great and the good. His son wasn't there, of course, and he wasn't David's firstborn, but he was special: so said the local priest, an old friend of David's with features like Gandalf and the prophetic ramblings to match. He'd baptised the boy, stared deep into his soul and pronounced him divinely anointed. David had been chuffed: only a year before he'd lost his previous child and the agony still burned like acid in his soul. But this son was a panacea – he'd want for nothing and David would make sure he'd become the brightest boy in the land.

As the twins grew up it became blindingly obvious – Jake and his brother Esau were different.

On Cain's fifth birthday his parents celebrated by dumping him with some friends he didn't know very well and rushing into hospital. He figured there'd be a proper party when they came back. There wasn't. Instead there

Beginnings

was a struggling new baby who now demanded all the attention: attention that had previously been given to him. Cain never recovered.

As the years passed it was clear that the new baby was favourite. Cain, the prototype, had been improved upon, and everybody seemed to consider mark two a vastly improved model. Cain tried his best but he couldn't help slipping further into the shadows, and in the semi-darkness he brooded on his misfortune and plotted ways to win back his parents' attention.

The hunt for *Black Hawk Down*

'Dad, why d'you stay in this dump?'

Sol's old man, Dave, had transformed a tiny council house into his own recording studio. A little neon sign hung in the modest top floor window intermittently sputtering and blinking the studio name, 'Radio Therapy Records'. The top floor was one single room, a jungle of speakers and cables, posters wilting off the walls like drooping palm leaves.

'Sol!' His dad was always pleased to see him. 'Listen, I got a new sound. Man, you won't believe this.'

Dave was a bulky guy, permanently tanned and criminally good looking. He wore his hair long, as if he was a roadie for Led Zeppelin and was an eternal optimist. He wore a smile most of the time; it was the kind of smile that exuded shedloads of charm.

He was at his desk, two huge 48-inch screens mounted on the wall in front of six dozen keys and sliders. He'd designed his own mixing desk and it looked like someone had smashed a Fisher-Price piano across the cockpit of a Boeing 747.

'It's massive, man. I have three groups in the download chart, and four more to follow.'

He pushed buttons and hiked sliders and the sound that exploded from the walls was like a jet taking off to the sound of a dozen saxophones and a hundred guitars.

'Admit it – you never heard this before, right?'

Sol's dad was sixty-three and lived like he was still fifteen.

'Dave, your curry's ready.'

Sol turned and stared at the blonde in the doorway. She was younger than him, with a perfectly proportioned face and more curves than a barrel of fruit, like something that had been designed for a web site. She smiled at Dave and disappeared again.

'Dad, who's that?' said Sol.

'Oh, just a friend. She's cutting a record.'

'And cooking you curry.'

When it came down to it, Sol's dad was an ageing rocker with a heart of gold and loins of clay.

'If I play my cards right I could soon have seven out of the top ten downloads. Seven! Check this out. I wrote it for Cliff – he's desperate for another number one. D'you see what I did with it?'

Dave passed his son a beer mat. Sol read the scribbled lyrics.

'I'm your Bachelor boy, you poor young ones, we don't talk any more you devil woman, O little town so wired for sound, your daddy's home and Carrie's my living doll.'

'It's terrible.'

'Better than his last one.'

'No, it's not, it's the worst idea you ever had. Doesn't even rhyme. Doesn't scan.'

His dad stared ahead at the complex bars of colour on the two screens. 'You wait, it'll go to number one,' he said.

'So? That proves nothing. Any crap does that these days. Who is she?'

'Who?'

'The girl. And why don't you get a bigger place? You're loaded. The people next door must be going nuts with the noise.'

'I am the people next door. I bought the house last week. What d'you think about getting him to do something with Meatloaf?'

'Who?'

'Cliff, keep your eye on the ball, will ya?'

'What, a sort of "Bat out of heaven" thing?'

His dad laughed. 'Yeah! Why not? I love you mate, you're great. You always were.' Without looking at him Dave reached out and squeezed his son's shoulder.

'So why did you spend so much time with other people?'

'What?' His dad looked genuinely shocked. As if they had not actually had this conversation a hundred times before.

'Dad, I know you think I'm the dog's biscuit, but the point is you can't just say that. I'm right here. Stop the music and give me some time.'

His father nodded solemnly, took his hands off the desk and swivelled his chair to face his son. 'Is it money again?'

'No.'

'A girl?'

'No, you're the one with the girl problems, Dad.'

'Dave! The curry!'

'Be right with you, babe.'

'Oh *babe*, is it?' said Sol.

'She's just a friend.'

'Have you seen Mum lately?'

Dave sighed. 'She won't talk to me.'

'Surprise surprise,' he muttered.

Sol glanced over at the pneumatic blonde who'd reappeared in the doorway.

'Dave,' she said.

'In a second babe, give us a minute, will ya?'

The pin-up girl rolled her eyes and slipped out. Sol's dad reached for his old mug, a massive cracked thing with Mink DeVille scrawled across it and a thousand chips embedded in the glaze. Sol's dad never washed his coffee mug: he just covered the stains with more stains. He took a slurp of something that looked like an oil leak and winced at the foul taste.

'She's got a degree, you know,' he said, nodding towards the door. 'I mean she's not a bimbo. Not at all. Not just bump and grind, she's . . .'

Sol raised an eyebrow and his dad threw up his hands.

'All right, Sol, listen. You're a smart lad – smarter than you deserve to be, and I got a problem. This boy band comes to me with a song they claim they've written – and it's brilliant. Will I produce it? Fine, I say, we'll sell a million. Next thing you know this girl band rolls up with an identical number, I mean identical, except all the "she"s have been changed to "he"s. And what d'ya know? They claim it's theirs. It's a brilliant song, but I haven't got a clue who wrote it. Neither of them registered it. But one of them pinched it.'

Sol blew out his cheeks and scratched his head. For a moment he was tempted to suggest they ask the pneumatic graduate. 'Scrap it,' he said.

'What?'

'Tell 'em you've found out they're lying, wave some document around that proves Billy Joel wrote it, a gas bill or something, and threaten to dump both bands.'

'What good will that do?'

'The band that didn't write it won't be bothered. They'll concede anything to stay with you. The band that did write it will be the ones that care. Trust me.'

'How d'you know these things?' Dave asked him.

'I dunno, obvious stuff. Hey, I've got a song – get Cliff to sing this one.' He searched in his pockets for a while. 'You haven't got my copy of *Gladiator* have you?' he asked as he pulled tenners and parking tickets from his jeans. 'And didn't I lend you *Black Hawk Down* as well?'

'Not sure. Maybe.'

'Here you go,' Sol slammed down a scrap of the cover of a movie magazine.

His father scrutinised it for a while. 'I can barely read this,' Dave said.

'That is me – that's where I'm at right now. From the heart.'

There was a sigh behind him and he turned to see the girl again.

He nodded at her and for the first time they made eye contact. Her eyes were different colours, one blue, one green. She smiled at him briefly. Somewhere in the background his father started reading the song.

'"There's a lime . . ."'

'*Time*. The word is *time*,' said Sol, dragging his eyes from the girl. '"There's a *time* for everything yet nothing ever changes."'

'Right – good line. "Time to live and die, love and hate, laugh and cry, watch and wait. Night and day, get and give away. Up, down, tear and mend, quiet, speak, start and end." Different. Not bad in fact, got a tune?'

'Course not,' said Sol, 'you're the music-meister.'

'Fair enough. "Build and plant, crash and burn, limp and dance, twist and turn . . ."'

Sol glanced back at her. Why did he do this? Why the sudden need to keep hooking her eyes with his, and why, oh, why did he get that sudden rush when he found she was waiting to lock her gaze on him? He felt an elbow in his ribs.

'I said . . . I don't like that bit.'

He turned back to his dad. He heard a footstep and glanced over his shoulder to see she'd gone. 'Has she got a sister?' he asked.

'No, and don't even go there. That's way too weird.'
'Why? She's only your cook.'
'Yeah . . . right . . . Look Sol, why are you thinking like this at your age? I mean the stuff in this song. You're twenty-seven, for heaven's sake. Your life's all there for you – youth and vitality – it should be all beer and football, not this gloom and doom.'

'Dunno . . . just feels like it goes round and round sometimes. Birth death, night day, wars ceasefires. Sometimes I just wake up at three in the morning and it all collides in my head like a massive traffic accident. Maybe I just had too much too soon.'

'What d'ya mean?'

'Well, great job, all the money I need, independence, quality of life. I've got it all, what else is there to live for? Maybe I should just give it away and start again. Do something different. Something weird, dangerous, radical.'

His dad stood up and put an arm around his shoulder.

'Oh oh, this isn't that bit where you show me your kingdom and tell me one day it'll all be mine?' said Sol.

His dad didn't laugh.

'You need a good woman, Sol,' he said.

'I can't – you've got 'em all.'

'Easy tiger. I can't help being a love machine. But look, I'm serious, life's about love and rock'n'roll . . . and God. What more d'you need?'

'Why's everything come down to sex, rock and religion with you, Dad?'

'You'll find out, mate. You can run but you can't hide.'

'Oh, I can run quite fast.'

'Good luck with that then.'

On his way out the front door he felt a hand on his shoulder. The grip was soft and small.

It was her.

She was offering him something. He stared at those eyes for a while, then she woke him up with one word.

'*Gladiator.*'

'What?'

Was it a compliment? She waved the plastic box in front of him.

'Oh yeah, right.' He glanced down at the DVD case.

'I heard you ask your dad for it. He's had it for months. Except it's not *Gladiator*. It's *Lord of the Rings*. You need to be more tidy.'

He took it. 'Thanks.' He'd had it for months? How did she know?

'I'll have to lend you the best movie in the world,' she said.

He nodded. He loved movies. Especially movies that brought him closer to the most beautiful girl in the world.

'See you next time.'

'Next time when?'

She smiled at him. 'Next time you visit your dad.'

'Oh right, yeah.'

She was way younger than him, so why did he suddenly feel like the little kid?

'You, er . . .' he licked his dry lips. 'You haven't got a sister, have you?'

She smiled again. 'No. Two brothers.'

'Oh. Right. Bye then.'

Sol spent the rest of his day thinking about her. And the rest of his week after that. Wherever he went she was there. Lurking in the background, hiding in the shadows of his thoughts. He couldn't escape. One encounter with this girl and he was trapped. Sol was like that. The *see something and want it* kid. It had worked with toys and gadgets. Wasn't quite so effective with women.

The snub

She picked up the black book and thumbed the pages. Those well-worn dockets of time: she loved that little black book. So much honesty, so much controversy, so much mystery.

Adam stood in the doorway. 'Haven't seen much of you lately.'

She looked up startled. 'Oh Dad, hi. Well, you know, been busy.'

'Miss you when you're not around.'

She smiled: a beautiful, heart-melting smile, one that began with her lips and ended with her eyes.

'I'll never stay away very long, Dad, and Cain's here.'

Adam scowled. 'Yeah well, could do with missing him a bit more . . .'

'Dad!'

'Well . . . he's so difficult sometimes, you know him. His mood swings are getting worse. Unbearable, at times.'

'You may not have to bear him at all soon: he's applied for a job, one away from here. Something in advertising . . .'

'Advertising? What's he know about that?'

'He'd be good, Dad. His heart's not in farming, especially after the Divine event last year.'

Adam shook his head and frowned bitterly. 'Was his own fault, didn't prepare properly, the boy was an idiot.

He's always been an idiot. Sometimes I wish I'd had two girls.'

Cain had stood beside his sister, nervously shifting from foot to foot. The presentation, held in the colossal ballroom of the Divine Hotel, was much bigger than expected. When he'd been asked to prepare and present a token of his work with his sister, he'd had no idea it would be like this. He'd pictured a shabby country church hall and a shabby country mayor wearing a chain off some old loo flush, not some royal dude, caviar and crab meat in a sparkling ballroom. This wasn't Cain's kind of thing at all. He shifted in his huge black boots, well aware that they hadn't been polished since they left the shop a long time ago. Sweat pooled in the small of his back as they waited for the royal nod and wink.

The room began to feel incredibly hot. Cain felt stupid in his Mohawk hairstyle, and his charity shop suit. Normally he loved this look but somehow it felt cheap and loud in this foreign setting. His stress levels went through the roof and he could feel his scalp start to prickle and itch, along with numerous eczema patches dotted around his body.

The nod and the wink were nodded and winked and the two of them shuffled forward. No, Cain shuffled, his sister glided effortlessly, and somehow they both crossed the red carpet and ended up in front of the fifteenth royal cousin twice removed. Some wrinkled prince the spitting image of Prince Philip, just older and without the charm.

He took one look at Cain and quickly moved onto his sister. Then Cain was left standing like an idiot while the other two conversed about the finer points of country life, climate and crab meat. Cain might well have not been there. In fact, shortly he wasn't – three minutes into the conversation he dumped his offering on top of a pile of tiramisu shaped like Windsor Castle and turned and left. He heard the cries from his dad and knew there'd be retribution, but he didn't care. He was fed up of looking an idiot. He'd been doing it all his life.

It was the last straw.

Abby

Abby was beautiful. There was no denying that. Men always turned to look in the street, women at parties shrank a little when she glided in. She was aware of it, of course, but never made it into some kind of weapon. Given the choice she'd be out in her wellies and cagoule, lumping soil about and shovelling dung. She got that from her dad. Her brothers took after their mum. But Abby was definitely Daddy's girl.

And she loved *Brief Encounter*. She had the deluxe version of the DVD, the special celebratory edition. She also had the mug and the poster. Every morning she woke up to Trevor ogling Celia in that plume of steam. She loved it. She couldn't get enough.

That subtle restraint; that frustrated, heart-rending, gut-wrenching desire; those moments of longing; that eighty-six minutes of green grass beyond the fence. That's what life was really made of, not the kind of thing they littered the screen with these days. Love left you bewildered and wrung out.

Abby was beautiful, but frustrated. That's why dung and soil were better than a million admirers. She had an appetite for life and nothing could satisfy it. So she threw herself into the earth, and celebrated whatever it threw back at her. She had no idea where the dull ache came from; she'd just always known it. In her teens she'd expected to find the answer, but as the years rolled by, and the opportunities came and went, she realised the hunger would never be met. She just had to live with it. She wanted more than life could offer. So instead she settled for what it put out there, whatever was in the shop window at any given moment. And in that she found a kind of happiness.

Just another concubine

Sol rolled over in bed and stared at the head on the pillow next to his. She had randomly scattered freckles on her perfect cheeks, lavish cherry-red lips and eyelashes that went on forever: a perfect magazine cover face. The gleaming white duvet was scrunched tightly around her body, like a layer of squirty cream garnishing a platter of fresh fruit. He just couldn't help seeing her like that. Sol had enjoyed that body all right. Her name was . . . He tried hard. He tried really hard. What was it? It began with 'E'. No, 'A'. No . . . Whoever she was, she stirred and rolled over and opened her eyes. Her cherry lips smiled dreamily at him and he smiled back. She was nine years younger than him. He remembered that. He even recalled the bar they met in and the smell of the taxi they took home. Home? His or hers? She smiled again and closed her eyelids slowly. Sol rolled onto his back and stared at the ceiling. Hers. Definitely hers. He didn't have a Barbie lampshade hanging from a pink ceiling. That was a relief. Not being his place made it very straightforward. Just slip out of bed and into his jeans in one easy movement. If she stirred he could whisper about nipping to the loo. He just wouldn't mention that it was his loo at his home without the pink paint and Barbie stuff. Wham bam and see you never again mam. He'd done it enough times lately. It was second nature now. It was a shame to leave this one. She was gorgeous.

Just another concubine

Any normal bloke would kill for a second date. But he wasn't normal. He was a man on a mission. A mission to bed enough girls to get that chick out of his system. His dad's green-eyed monster. The babe who cooked curry, recorded songs and slept with his old man. Argggh! Slept with his old man? How could she do that? Why would she want to? He had a body like Worzel Gummidge. Why? Why?

'Sol?'

Damn. He'd wasted time thinking about another woman, this one was waking up and starting to demand stuff from him. Fresh coffee, breakfast in bed, the next six months of his life. He could see it coming right at him.

'I . . . I just gotta take a leak . . .'

'Don't be gone long, I'm off work all day.'

'Well, give me a minute. I'll be right back.'

'Oh, Sol . . .'

'Honest, I'll be right back.'

And he was gone. Out of bed, across the carpet, bundling his clothes together as he went. Out of the bedroom, turn left down the hall, oops, nope, wrong way, that was her loo, he didn't want her loo, quick, back down the hall, kitchen, lounge, mind that pile of DVDs, undo the chain, out the front door. Perfect. He'd even dressed on the way. He was out of her flat and taking the stairs three at a time before she could call out to him one last time.

Out in the street he stopped to watch the TVs in the department store. He watched as a bank clerk shook his head miserably and held up an empty safe deposit box, then an old guy popped up on the screen making some impassioned appeal about the story; and then a tall, pot-bellied, big-haired vicar mouthed at the world about some old table he was sitting on, before a familiar face popped up on the screen and Sol grinned at the sight of his dad — the old rogue was winning yet another gold disc for something or other. All in glorious 48-inch widescreen. The people were bigger than he was. Sol shook his head. What was the point? The world went round and round, nothing changed. He recoiled as 48 inches of famine vomited at him out of the screen without warning. Babies with fluffy hair and distended stomachs screamed silently while their salty tears attracted flies. Armed men in sunglasses hijacked food trucks at roadblocks and everyone's misery went on. The world turned but each revolution was just like the last. The spinning globe never got anywhere. He wished he could boot it into oblivion and put the victims and villains out of their misery. Instead he went home and made himself fresh coffee and bagels.

Twenty minutes of curiosity

Dave poured himself a Dutch beer, slumped at his mixing desk and began flicking at the sliders. He had a slack morning and slack mornings always led to too much beer. It happened from time to time these days – he'd always steered clear of the drugs, but now boredom clawed at his door and he staved off the grey spectre with an alcohol injection. He glanced around the studio; that's when he noticed the book. A little black leather-bound volume. Someone had left it under the Clash poster, the famous one with Paul Simonon smashing his guitar on stage. Dave scooped up the book and crashed back down in front of his desk. He put on his latest signing, Madonna-to-Mud, and started thumbing through it. Page after page ushered in scenes to his mind, events long forgotten of his life of derring-do. Dave hadn't always been a record producer. Oh no. He'd seen plenty of action in his time, as a commando, a mercenary, a fugitive and even king of his own little bit of Africa for a while. Until he spied his neighbour's wife across the kraal one night and, while the poor schmuck neighbour was out on safari, he'd invited her round and wrecked everybody's lives. All for twenty minutes of curiosity. He cracked open another beer and ventured a little further into the book. He loved the songs in those fragile pages, could have written them himself. Angst and agony, hopes and horror. If only he could find a boy writer that could pen stuff like this today. Too much of your *yeah, yeah I really love you baby* and not enough of *this broken world turns and with every revolution it puts another crack in my heart*. It crossed his mind that he'd not passed enough of this wisdom on to Sol. He'd make sure he did. Just as soon as he'd downed another beer and snuggled up to the latest young thing in his bed.

Mosher

Jake flipped open the CD and heard an ominous crack. Stupid cases. They all had that same fatal flaw, wafer-thin hinges weaker than a wishbone.

He turned to the CD player – but it was no longer there, someone had replaced it with his old Dansette record player, the one encased in the blue box that he used to sit on when he was fourteen; those days of listening to *Give 'Em Enough Rope* by the Clash over and over and over again. How could he play a CD on a turntable? It just wasn't possible. You couldn't do it.

He looked about for something vinyl to put on the deck but there were no records in the studio. Sunset Radio Smile 2375 didn't accommodate vinyl. It was just a small town station with a couple of CD players, a mini disc and a hard drive. Mosher the tech guy had no truck with vinyl. He just thought it was some kind of paint. Jake glanced through the huge single pane of soundproofed glass that looked out over the office. Mosher was there, sitting at his desk surrounded by keyboards and cables and chocolate. Jake glanced at the clock. 5.55 pm, only five minutes to the show. He stepped up to the studio window and waved at Mosher. No response. Mosher didn't even look up.

Jake bashed on the glass but of course the sound didn't travel. He yelled, he screamed, he beat the window until his knuckles started to ooze blood. Red smears appeared on the glass. Streaks slashed across it like bright crimson wounds. Mosher finally glanced up and grinned at him. Then he went back to work. How could he do that? 5.57 pm. Jake threw himself back onto the leather swivel chair. There had to be some vinyl somewhere. He pulled open drawers and pushed aside books and files. It had to be here somewhere. 5.58. A little mountain of paper, cardboard CDs and dirty Styrofoam cups was beginning to form on the floor around him. He was sitting in the middle of his own rubbish heap. It had to be here . . . 5.59. Ah. Yes. At last. That old Queen album. The one with 'Killer Queen' on it. He could play that and leave it running while he started the show and went looking for Mosher.

He scooped up the purple cover and tipped out the white inner sleeve. Inside the paper was the precious disc. He placed it on the turntable and flicked the slider. Nothing. There was an air-splintering click, about the volume of a gunshot, as the clock flicked to 6.00 pm. He was on air. He was live. It was his show now. Desperately he flicked the catch again. Nothing. He gripped the cable and followed it under the desk to the wall. The cable went on and on – it was way too long for that matchbox studio. He began gathering it in his arms, and all the while there was the sound of silence. The one not made by Simon & Garfunkel. The one that was death to any DJ, and if not death then certain unemployment.

The cable was going on forever: miles of it, piling up so high on his lap it was beginning to crush his hopes.

Suddenly here was Mosher. Coming to his rescue. Only it wasn't Mosher. It was like him – but different. Like someone had put him into a computer programme and messed about with him. His head was massive. Mosher had an unusually large head anyway, but nothing this big. And his hands had grown too: they were like two piles of raw meat. One of them curled up into a fist and came through the air at him. Jake dodged, but then a second blow caught him on the cheek and made his head spin.

'Mosher! What are you doing? I need help here.'

Crack, another hit to his chin. Jake began to feel sick. He stood up, his vision blurred, the studio rotating like a rogue dodgem car.

'Mosher, stop hitting me.'

But Mosher wouldn't, instead he thumped Jake on the shoulder, then head-butted him in the chest and kneed him in the groin. Jake spasmed and fell backwards, all the air exploding from his lungs. He expected to land in the swivel chair any minute, but it wasn't there. He fell and fell and eventually the hard floor rose up and smacked him on the back of the head. Mosher leapt on him and the guy weighed a ton; it was like hugging an articulated lorry. They rolled around for a while on the floor. Mosher seemed to have gained the strength of another ten techie guys. He was going to throttle Jake if Jake didn't do something. Jake flailed around for a while then at last his hand found the base of an Anglepoise lamp. He clutched it and brought it crashing down on Mosher's oversized head. It was enough to make Mosher loosen his grip. Jake rolled free and stood up, kicking Mosher in the side as he did. Mosher gasped and clutched his body. Jake stood over him.

'Mosher, we're on air. It's my show,' he gasped. 'I've only got a turntable.'

Mosher sat up, spat on the carpet and slammed his sledgehammer fist into the tiny space between Jake's eyes. Jake felt himself falling, blacking out as he went.

Then he sat up in bed. As usual he was covered in sweat. Same old dream. Same old wrestling match. When would it end? He always woke up exhausted from these nightmares, as if he'd been wrestling with God.

Jake glanced at the clock. It was three in the morning. He got up and prepared for his show.

Giants and de‿

Dave had spent three hours at the mixing desk, 'Strike my feet' by Madonna-to-Mud had been on repeat play and was just coming round for the twenty-third time. He couldn't tear himself away from the adventures of his namesake. The Lord's anointed one gets a quick coronation, kills a giant and then what d'you know? Finds himself living rough surrounded by losers and vagabonds. Dave smiled ruefully; he'd toppled a few giants in his time. Rival companies intent on swallowing up all the talent and spewing it out for cheap profit. He'd stood his ground and seen them all off. It had taken nerve and courage and a lot of hard-learned tricks, but his skills had paid off, and there was no doubt the Boss up there had seen him through it all. Some people seemed to think living was about saying your prayers and expecting the world to land on your plate. Not Dave – he'd always grabbed life by both hands and wrestled it to the ground – sweat, toil, cuts and bruises – that had been his story. And plenty of heartfelt pleas hurled at the blood-red sky as he fought on. Occasionally when he stopped and looked back he could see the footprints of God in the sand, the Boss beside him in the good and the bad. And like this biblical king, Dave had mastered his trade in the wild places. Africa and Asia, heat and dust and flies: that's where he'd learnt to be a sharp businessman and an astute leader. In the dry places of life.

The victim

'Jake.'

It was Mosher.

'Your victim's here.'

'He's not a victim, he's a guest.'

'He's not who I think he is, is he?'

Jake rolled his eyes. 'No, not if you think he's Brad Pitt.'

'No,' Mosher gave a toothy grin. 'That record producer bloke, the one who had a go at Pete Waterman on Jonathan Ross.'

'Just send him in, will you?'

Jake slid a few sliders, punched a few buttons and got into character. Dave King was not a guest to be trifled with – once the biggest-selling producer in the land, and despite his age, still soldiering on, refusing to roll over and let the young dudes steal his crown.

'Mr King, welcome to the show.'

'Call me Dave.' The king smiled and nodded and didn't waste his time on too many words.

'Thanks for making the trip. Good journey over?'

'Yup, fine. I've been catching up with a few new bands and some old flames.'

Jake shuffled papers and tried to look in control. This was Dave King. *The* Dave King. Opposite him, in his studio. On his show.

'I'll just play out this tune and then we'll have a natter,' Jake said.

The Victim

He put on The Spoilt View and Dave laughed. 'These lads came to me, you know.'

'Really?'

'Yeah, I was on a bad day. Missed a good thing there.'

More shuffling papers. Jake didn't need to shuffle them; he just needed time to calm his nerves in the presence of greatness.

'Good of you to come on the show.'

'I listen. Better than Mr Wright.'

'Really?' Jake felt his cheeks hotting up.

'Yeah, not Mr Evans though. Who could beat the boy wonder?'

Jake frowned. He was trying, he was trying. The Spoilt View wound up with a searing scream that probably lost a few listeners, and Jake introduced Dave.

They chatted on air about past glory and future conquests and then Jake slipped on Dougal and the Diggers, a long-forgotten one-hit wonder band.

'Should have had a second single,' Dave lamented with a pained frown. 'I let 'em go too soon. Dougal's cleaning toilets now you know? Got his own sewage firm. Sad but true.'

'How's the family these days?' Jake asked.

Dave looked a little startled. 'Scattered,' he said. 'Apart from one. My youngest lad. But you knew him, didn't you?'

'Went to school with him.'

The song wound up and they chatted some more on air.

'Now Dave, one of the stories that's always perplexed me about you . . .'

'Oh oh, what's coming now?'

Jake laughed and raised a hand. 'Don't worry, it's nothing like that.'

'Like what?'

Dave eyeballed the young DJ for a moment. Jake glanced around for a spade. He was gonna have to start digging if this went on much longer. Silence seemed to fill the studio like tear gas. Jake was frozen, a rabbit in Dave King's headlights. Then Dave's face cracked and he laughed.

'Go on,' he said, with melodramatic caution in his voice.

Jake began slowly. 'Your studio – Radio Therapy – it's just a little caravan on a bit of waste ground. You're phenomenally successful: why don't you have a mansion on a hill somewhere?'

Dave nodded slowly and pursed his lips. He placed a little black book on the desk and withdrew a cigarette packet from his pocket. For a moment Jake panicked at the thought of having to reprimand the great Dave King about the indoor smoking laws live on air. Dave pulled out a smoke, then thought better of it and stuck it behind his ear for later.

'Jack . . .' he said.

Jake was slightly miffed about that one.

'Sorry.' Dave grinned for a second and held up an apologetic hand, '*Jake*, you know it's always been about the music for me. Someone once said "Wait till you outgrow your vision before you start building something bigger". I actually have something far grander than a caravan – couple of semi-detached houses. I'm planning to expand but – maybe I'll leave that to the next generation. I have a hunch my son will do the new build – not me. He has a bigger vision . . . a bigger appetite, let's say. I'm happy to rattle out a couple of new bands and a number one single every so often. I like that.'

Dave absentmindedly took the cigarette from behind his ear and flicked his disposable lighter. Jake waited till he'd put on a little-known Bowie track and faded the mics before sheepishly apprehending him.

'Not many people know you produced this song, Dave,' he added breezily.

The big man shrugged and jabbed a sunburnt finger across the desk.

'If a song is great you don't have to do that much to it,' he said. 'I wish I could say I produced the famous Bowie numbers, but I never got offered them.'

'Good book?' Jake said, pointing at the black book.

'I found it the other day in my studio,' Dave said. 'It's a friend's. Borrow it if you want; she won't mind.'

Jake reached over, took it and thumbed through. He smiled wistfully.

'Been a long time, used to have one of these when I was little. You forget.'

It'd be something to announce that the legendary Dave King had lent him a book. Not quite so impressive that it was a Bible he didn't even own.

'Might just hang onto it for couple of days,' said Jake. 'If you don't mind?'

Dave shook his head. 'Plenty of songs in there to go nicking,' he said. 'A mine of untapped genius. Spent three hours just the other day poring over it with a crate of beer.'

Beer in one hand and a Bible in the other. Not quite the image he had in mind of the great Dave King. Jake smiled again and slipped the book into the pocket of his graffitied denim jacket.

Mo Mountain

Like many affable guys, Jake put on a good show in public: the nice dude front. Only in private did he let out his real feelings and any bubbling anger that had begun to fester inside during his day. Some people thought him the nicest guy on the planet. But he knew better. A couple of glasses of Jack Daniels and he was ready to kill anybody who got in his way.

His encounter with Dave King had left him with surprisingly mixed feelings. Being in the presence of greatness had warmed his soul and left him strangely humbled.

Yet the great presence clearly had hidden shallows, and a memory like a sieve. Jack? Jack? Surely the big guy could have had the decency to remember his name!

Jake lived in a converted church, a gaunt crag of a building on the edge of the moor. Bethel Chapel sat in its own tiny burial ground, a few slabs of stone rising from the turf like the torsos of the dead. On misty evenings Jake sat in the porch smoking a cheroot and watching the fifteenth-century shadows cavort around ancient graves. A right old haunted house on hallowed ground. He'd heard that Hammer had once considered the place for a battleground between Dracula and Van Helsing.

Back home that night, Jake poured a third Jack Daniels and took it outside. He kicked a few of the graves, then thought better of it. Instead he stood in the centre of the dead and howled like a wolf. Anyone would have thought him mad, but Jake often howled on his own: it wasn't unusual for him to wave a fist at the sky and rant and rave into the unknown. He'd never do it to another earthly being, so he might as well let it all out at the heavenly ones.

When he was exhausted from the shouting he fell back against his favourite tomb, a craggy epitaph to a long dead hero. Mo Mountain – 'He lived with God on his shoulder' – so the stone said. What did that mean? Was it a threat or a promise? Intimacy or tyranny? Could you know the unknowable so well it felt as if he were a mate in a rugby scrum, or even better, a fellow reveller at a New Year's gig? *He lived with God on his shoulder.* Jake's problem was he felt a little like that, but the experience was not a good one. As he sat there now he glanced back, just once. Just to wonder again if the Great Man were really there, bearing down on him. Watching his every move, waiting to pounce and pummel him for his many misdemeanours. Like a bad father.

His dad often spoke of a good father: Jake's granddad, Abraham. But to Jake, his own dad had increasingly seemed distant and divorced from him. Esau was the good son, the apple of his dad's eye. Jake was nothing more than the speck in his mother's.

Rebekah was an astute woman, she knew how to handle Jake's dad, she always had. Ever since that first day when they bumped into each other in that churchyard. Strange place to start a relationship, but Isaac was broken up over the loss of his mother and Rebekah was a good listener. They'd been together ever since.

Rebekah knew how to handle Jake too, they had plenty of common ground. But not Esau. Esau wasn't tender enough, not malleable to her will and whim. So she concentrated on little Jake. And Jake became a chip off the maternal block. He was charming like his mother. She could smile and smile and yet be a villain. She wouldn't have been surprised to find Jake out here shrieking amongst the stones: she'd have been there with him.

'What's all the noise?'

He leapt up and stared at the door. It was Leah. Half-naked and with a guitar in one hand.

'I thought you were out tonight?' he said.

'I felt sick so I stayed in.'

'You're always ill at the moment. What's going on?'

'I'm OK. Was it you howling?'

He blushed and swiped at Mo Mountain's Rock. 'Nope. Well, yeah, sort of. Just getting something out of my system. I met Dave King today.'

'Great,' she said.

And she turned and went back inside.

The black book

Jake clicked on the playlist for his show and scowled. Why did the computer have such bad taste? Human beings were no longer permitted to choose the music that fed love. Now a heartless piece of kit with nothing but a motherboard and hard drive had control of the airwaves, Jake's show was planned by a computer – a robot without a soul. Jake opened a beer and did what he always did: he pulled out his memory stick, jammed it into the USB port and downloaded his own music of choice. If the bosses complained he'd just say what he always said: the mighty machine must have glitched. Gone were the overblown anthems of the eighties and the soulless techno of the nineties. Instead the playlist bulged with the likes of Nirvana, Stiff Little Fingers, Wreckless Eric, Covert Kisses, Antrim Phoenix, Duck-billed Satirist and the Byrds. And his one concession to the cheese of the seventies in the form of 'Daydream Believer' by the Monkees.

He waited while the news ended and the weather kicked in, pacing up and down inwardly as the adrenalin began to kick in and jolt him into character. A quick advert for Twice Shy double glazing then the Ramones fired up their guitars and he was off. He eased a couple of sheets of A4 from his jeans, folded triple and covered in doodles and smudges. These were tonight's stories; tonight's tales of life and love gleaned from that day's skulking in coffee shops and bus shelters: tales he was sure would set the airwaves alight.

He opened a can of Coke and hoiked out the book Dave King had lent him. The Ramones finished up and he let the Shins take the reins, saying the bare minimum of welcomes so as not to ruin the great happy jangling of the boys as they got going. Then he scooped up the book and flicked through its pages.

It was pretty battered, with coffee stains, ink spatters and . . . was that nail varnish flecked across the pages? Grief, this had seen some action. He slurped some drink, a few fizzy droplets showering across the book in his hand, adding to the tapestry.

Back and forth he flicked, trying to work out the language. It was English, but somehow the words were like another dialect. As if an Afrikaner were trying to speak Dutch. He concentrated and tried again. He was concentrating so hard he almost missed the end of the Shins. He realised in the nick of time that the boys were finishing up and someone else needed to take over. He panicked and did the strangest thing: he told the truth.

'Just got distracted there by a strange little book here on the desk. Full of names and lists and words – even got mine in it. I'll leave you in the capable hands of Scouting for Girls and I'll be right back with a little wisdom for ya.'

Scouting for Girls took longer than they should have to get their capable hands on the airwaves but they got there eventually and Jake could turn his attention back to the leather-bound book.

It was true. He was right there in those pages. Or if not him, someone who sounded a helluva lot like him. Some guy at a river who turned in for the night and then got mugged by a stranger. The image of the fight round the camp-fire took Jake back to those days of crouching in front of the TV watching old cowboy movies from the fifties with his dad. Long drawn-out affairs that occasionally lapsed into excitement in the form of smoking gun battles or dusty knife fights in the shadows of flickering camp-fires. It was heady stuff: back then and now. Jake leafed backwards and found his namesake was always on the run, dreaming dreams and seeing visions and picking up women at wells. And – weird – the guy's old man was called Isaac too. He shivered and dropped the book as the Girl Scouters began to wind down.

'So all you average punters out there,' (he always called them that, his subversive way of challenging the station's notion that somehow there actually existed a punter out there who was in any way *average*) 'I have this weird tome in my hot little rock'n'roll fingers and bizarrely enough – it's all about me! Yup – I kid you not. Ever read a book where you flipped open the pages and came across your name – well, course you have – but how about if your own name appeared alongside your dad's name too? Yup – that'd make you sit up in your average seat and turn up your average volume button.'

He cued up Reel Big Fish and set them off crooning about New York. He also lined up Zulu Prawn, Stan & Ollie and Madonna-to-Mud to follow to give him some thinking time.

He turned a few more pages and found his eyes wandering across spidery text about some young punk running away from his family. Ouch! That hurt. Apparently the guy threw everything that belonged to him, and plenty that didn't, into a rucksack and took off into the unknown. Then he just kept partying like there was no tomorrow, until there really was no tomorrow, and he found himself dying and alone in the gutter. Well, Jake wasn't that badly off just yet, in fact he was doing pretty nicely thanks. But then, unlike this prodigal punk in the black book, he hadn't spent his days partying: he'd been out getting the job of a lifetime. And it was paying dividends.

He flipped back, skipping endless lists of people spending an awful lot of happy time begetting. Then he found himself wading through a jungle of knowledge, paragraph after paragraph of short pithy proverbs. Now this was more his style.

'Happy is the guy who acquires wisdom and gets understanding.' He read the line aloud to himself.

That made sense, sounded good on the ear, that was worth noting down for some future soundbite moment on his show.

'Do not withhold good from those who deserve it when it's in your power to help them.'

Noble. A good one for a quick thought for the day.

'I listen carefully to many proverbs and solve riddles with inspiration from a harp.'

Now that was perfect for a music and talk show. Could almost be his strap line.

He went on reciting, enjoying the sound of his own voice.

'It's possible to give freely and become more wealthy, but those who are stingy will lose everything.'

'The generous prosper and are satisfied; those who refresh others will themselves be refreshed.'

He scribbled these last two down – in fact he scribbled a lot for quite a while. This little book of wisdom could give him plenty of urban acumen to slip between his favourite tunes. And that's what Jake's life was about – soundbite wisdom and three-minute pop songs. Nothing else mattered.

'Are you going mental or what?' It was Mosher, he'd heard the reciting and was worried.

'It's OK, mate,' Jake said. 'Just practising a bit of wisdom.'

Mosher rolled his eyes. 'Mental,' he said again, but he left, shutting the door behind him.

'Good people enjoy the positive results of their words, but those who are treacherous crave violence.' Now wasn't that just the difference between him and his brother?

'Those who follow crooked paths will slip and fall.' Oh. Was that some kind of warning?

The little black book was starting to spook him. He wrote down a few more nuggets then stuck it in a jiffy bag, addressed it, and put it in the office post tray. Dave King at Radio Therapy Records was welcome to it, thanks very much.

Jake pulled on his denim jacket. It had an elaborate design on the back: the cover of *Give 'em enough rope* drawn in black and red pen; something he'd done on one of the many nights while he'd lain awake in Bethel Chapel, fearing what his brother might do to him if he ever found him. He'd seen Esau loosen wheel nuts on artic lorries with his bare hands. He'd make short work of throttling Jake; there was no doubting that.

The edge of everything

Jake hadn't always lived out here in the wild; he was really a child of suburbia, but after a bust-up with his brother and a reprehensible incident with his old man, he'd chucked a few things into his university rucksack and jumped on a bus. Literally. Just enough time to pack the essentials such as toothpaste, underwear, iPod, wallet, his laptop and that extremely rare limited-edition Clash single. That was about a year ago, and that day of leaving had been the worst twenty-four hours of his life. He should have gone back with a simple 'sorry' on his tongue: but no, the men in his family were all way too stiff-necked for that kind of behaviour. However, now he'd found Bethel Chapel, struck a deal, done it up and started again. Life was back on the up.

Just down the lane and across the road was The Ladder. It claimed to be number one in the top ten best-pub-view chart, and he believed it because, let's face it, when would he ever get around to checking the other nine?

It was pretty good inside too: served real ale, tasty fresh food, and had a gang of gigantic brown-leather, overstuffed, saggy-armed, body-hugging sofas. He could describe them so well because he had intimate and regular contact with the things. Except for the nights when Rach was around. Rach wasn't allowed in the Ladder because of the smell. Her smell, not the pub's. Rach

The edge of everything

drank way too much of the kind of stuff you couldn't get over the counter at The Ladder. She wore a baggy metal-green shell suit with tears and rips in it and a Ramones T-shirt underneath. She and Jake had one thing in common. They were both on the run. Jake had his craggy chapel. Rach slept in a disused hut half a mile from the pub. Very few people slept rough in that neck of the woods and she knew she'd have to move on sooner or later. But Rach had the kind of history that kept her away from city streets and cardboard bedrooms under bridge arches. The city was too violent, too reminiscent of a twisted extended family.

The nights when Rach showed up with her two Sainsbury's bags, her oil-stained sleeping bag and her scuffed backpack were Jake's favourites. Rach was gorgeous. Underneath the scars and the muck and the food stains, she was the most beautiful girl Jake had ever seen. If the B.O. and booze had been replaced by Chanel No. 5 she'd have had men falling over her most nights. Instead, she fell over most nights, and most men didn't even see her when they walked past. If they did notice it was only the smell. She didn't care. Well . . . she did, who wouldn't have cared about having to sleep in a shite-stained bag, in an old signalman's hut near a disused rat-infested bit of railway track? But what she didn't care about was the lack of men. Men had done plenty to her and that would last her the rest of her life. Except for Jake. Against her better judgement she liked Jake and was starting to believe he liked her. Though there was no telling how far a bloke might deceive you to get inside your underwear. Even if you did smell bad.

Rach was sitting there now, on the bit of turf beneath the line of copper beech trees, her chaotic red hair busting out beneath her baseball cap, like flames from a collapsing building. She always sat there, hunched up like a pile of rotting compost. It was far enough from the pub to get away with it, and the brow gave the brilliant view of the wild moor and the mad ponies below. The ponies were mad. Definitely. They acted like teenagers on speed. And the beauty of it was – they didn't care who knew it. Rach had a wild pony like that inside her. That's why she loved watching them go bananas.

As Jake stepped up she threw him a nervous glance, worried at first; she was always worried about people. She smiled when she saw it was him.

Before Rach had been old and homeless she had been young and a DJ. Her dad owned a huge garden with a crappy old shed at the bottom of it that never got used so she filled it with vinyl. She had everything by everyone. She loved that shed, until her uncle followed her there one night and turned it into a house of pain. Bastard.

Jake knew all this: he knew plenty about her because they spent long nights sitting chatting on the brow looking at the ponies. He bought her legitimate drinks and she told him about music. He fuelled her habit and she fuelled his show. She was twenty-five.

What made things more complex was the relationship Jake had with Leah, Rach's sister. It was complex because Rach and Leah had no idea about the Jake factor in each other's lives.

Jake and Leah weren't strictly dating. They were doing everything else though. Regularly. And Leah often 'stayed over'. There was just no framework to the thing. It was the relationship that dared not speak its name. Because it didn't have one. Leah didn't dare name it in case it gave Jake the heebie-jeebies. Jake didn't dare name it because of his guilt over the fact of knowing both sisters but admitting it to neither. And because it would give him the heebie-jeebies.

Leah had also ended up on the street, but in a different sense. She was a full-time busker. She may not have had the face of an angel – Rach had that – but Leah had the voice.
Jake had met Leah about six weeks ago.

About six weeks ago

Jake walked into the town centre and in spite of the jangling musical cheese oozing from the shops and the cafés he heard the guitar before he heard anything else. Then he heard her voice. And Tracy Chapman's 'Behind the wall'.

It took him a while to spot the tall figure in the leather coat and Union Jack trousers, but once he spotted her he couldn't stop looking. He went closer. She paused for breath and then Alanis Morissette's 'Ironic' tumbled from her lips. Long thin dark lips, on a mouth as broad as Minnie Driver's. Not stunning, but a mystery. And with the clearest blue eyes in the world. So he sat on the bench and listened. And twenty minutes later he shuffled up and chatted to her and tried to coerce her into coming on his show to play live. Right after trying to coerce her into coming to his home so they could both play live. She didn't trust him but they went and had coffee – him espresso, her strawberry latte – and it went from there.

Eight days later she moved some of her stuff into Bethel Chapel. He only discovered she was Rach's sister four weeks later.

He and Rach were sitting on the brow discussing music when she mentioned Tracy Chapman and Alanis Morissette. It was too much of a coincidence; he couldn't help mentioning the girl in the square with the divine voice and Union Jack trousers. Rach snorted.

'Sounds as bad as my sister,' she said and proceeded to describe Leah to the last detail.

'Anyway,' she finished up. 'What about that girl in the square? What's her name? You shagging her then?'

'Er . . .' The penny was still dropping as she finished speaking, and thinking on his backside was never Jake's strong point, despite his job as a live radio presenter. He put in a lot of preparation so he could sound that spontaneous on air.

'Er . . . the girl in the square? She's called, er . . . L . . . Le . . . Le–ucy.'

'Lee–ucy?'

'Yeah. Funny name, eh?'

'Bet she sings better than my sister.'

'Oh, I wouldn't say that.'

'She's probably better looking.'

'I wouldn't say that.'

Rach turned and frowned at him, she had a streak of mud across her chin and a fresh graze above her right eye. Her eyes looked darker and more deeply-set than ever.

'What would you say, Mr Loverman?'

'I . . . I'm going to get her on my show. Which means . . . she'll be a star one day.'

Rach sniffed. 'That'll screw her up then. Fame's bad for your health. Leah wants to be famous. Stupid cow. She'll be playing outside Sainsbury's for the rest of her life.'

'Smith's actually.'

'What?'

'Nothing. I'll get you another drink.'

The back of beyond

Sol pulled up in his Maserati and clambered out. He was in the back of beyond, some little village out in the sticks. He often did this, drove until he found some anonymous pub in some anonymous backwater. Somewhere to spend a few hours with a couple of pints and a local girl. It was his way of escaping.

He stepped onto the path leading up to the ivy-decked door then froze when he heard the dogs. Somewhere in this place there were Alsatians, at least a couple, and Sol had a pathological fear of those things – ever since an incident from those days when he was small enough for such creatures to tower above him like velociraptors. He had once come home from school to find a couple of them on the loose in his street and had to run for cover through neighbours' gardens, hopping over walls and ducking under hedges to escape their razor fangs. To make matters worse one of them had left a huge mountain of faeces in their drive, and the first Sol knew of this was when he looked at his footprints on the carpet and realised he'd trodden the stuff halfway round the house. Not a good day. Not a good day at all. And it came back to him every time he heard that familiar snarling sound. No bevy of local beauties could make this little hostelry worth his while.

Then he saw her. The landlady. Not some young impressionable wench, but a tough thirty-something

Boadicea, with steel in her eyes and acid for blood. The challenge was too much.

'Quiet, Ammo!' she snapped from the doorway. Then she spotted Sol and gave him a raised eyebrow. 'Nice car,' she said and he grinned like a schoolboy.

'Those dogs gonna maul me?' he asked.

She shook her head briefly. 'Not if you got plenty of money to spend.'

Maybe it was because he was tired of his preoccupation with his dad's girl, maybe it was just because he was Sol. Either way in that moment he found her irresistible, and in a pub with no customers there was plenty of opportunity to weave his charm.

'I'm not gonna sleep with you,' she said eventually, as they supped pints in the low-ceilinged bar. 'I know your kind, wide boys with fast cars and fire in your trousers. D'you think I don't get this every week?'

He shrugged. 'It's always worth a try. Hey. Ever seen *Brief Encounter*?'

She grimaced. 'I have a mate who had a Saturday job in an underwear shop called that.'

He laughed. 'Right. Well, I have a mate who claims it's the best movie in the world.' He still couldn't get his dad's girlfriend out of his head.

'So?'

'So that's what this is. You and me. Two worlds colliding for a split second of infinity. Shame to waste it.'

She gave him a forced smile. 'Look, I've never seen the film and I'm not in the mood for your chat up. All right?'

He shrugged. He could take 'no' for an answer.

He pulled a little black card from his jeans and she snorted.

'Oh here we go. "Call me next time you're cold and lonely."'

'Saves me having to say it. But if nothing else you should watch *Brief Encounter*.'

'I don't have it.'

'That's perfect. 'Cause one day I'm gonna roll up with a copy in my pocket.'

'As long as that's all you've got in there.' She winked and strolled away.

He downed his pint, gave her a wave and left his card on the bar.

The packet

Sol's main problem with life was simple. Boredom. He got an idea, threw himself at it like Spiderman to a wall, then halfway through fell off and limped off to find something new to attack. Whenever he found something, he stuffed himself so full of it that the newness quickly faded and it was no longer interesting any more. He had a big appetite. It had been there all through growing up. Fishing, pets, bikes, air guns, model planes. Whatever his latest passion, he couldn't rest until he owned it and had everything associated with it and then, having consumed it, he immediately tired of it.

And now it was the same story with women.

He found the packet on his doormat. It was waiting for him when he got home. He tore it open with the kind of fervour only associated with unexpected post and intriguing Christmas presents. Then he sat there on the hall carpet in his apartment, staring at the little black book. Who'd sent him this? It wasn't even new. It had blotches and stains on the cover. There were so many different shades the leather looked like a map of Africa. It was well thumbed and frayed at the edges, like something you'd find in the bargain section of a second-hand bookshop. The kind of thing no one else was likely to buy.

He flicked open the cover and immediately recognised the writing. It was from his father.

Sol, read this and weep, Dave.

Yet again it struck him. The name.
Dave, not *Dad* like most fathers. *Dave. Famous Dave. Radio Therapy Dave.*

Sol began to rifle the pages. The typeface was small and densely packed. It was not exactly Tony Parsons. He dug a little deeper and immediately found something about sex. Typical. He often managed to stumble across something inappropriate somewhere. You weren't supposed to open up the good book and start reading about lips and breasts and legs. He read on and found an ageing fifty-something monarch feeling all insecure about abandoning his troops to war. The frustrated hero is standing there gawping out of his bedroom window whilst a girl half his age strips off and takes a bath on a roof. Sounded just like his old man. I bet the roof babe had green and blue eyes, he thought, and that set him off thinking about his old man's girl again.

He flicked away and found a hundred proverbs. No sign of any birds and bushes but plenty of stuff about avoiding pride, prejudice and prostitutes. Logical if uncompromising. Then he found something that made his blood run cold. Some wide boy going by the name of Solomon (the very same guy in fact who was busy expounding on the danger of loose women) was getting all bored with his life and had started filling the void with as many subservient wives and ripe concubines as possible. A thousand women in fact. How would you remember their names? Well, clearly he didn't, 'cause none of them were recorded in the black book. None of them. A thousand women and no names. That wasn't good at all. You'd be just getting down to business, getting all passionate and unrestrained with the latest flame and before you know it you'd start panting the name of

The packet

the wench from a week last Wednesday. Undoubtedly the absolute quickest way to pour water on a raging fire. It'd be a slap in the face and no last tango in Paris for you, mate.

Sol shivered: it was too close for comfort. Books were supposed to be the great escape, not the tight corner that made you feel hemmed in. No book had the right to mirror your own life. Especially one with more blemishes than his old man. He shut it and took it into the kitchen. He loaded up the cafetière and carried both to the lounge. Black leather furniture littered the place like overgrown idle panthers. He threw himself at the nearest chair and gulped his coffee. Why would his old man send him this? What was he trying to tell him? The phone rang. Sol picked it up and dropped the Bible. He couldn't believe it. It was the most beautiful girl in the world. That made him feel better, and he forgot about the parcel for a while.

The best movie in the world

He met her in a coffee shop in the city and they laughed a lot. She was easy to talk to and she spoke his language.

'What are you doing here?' he asked after a while. 'I mean, why did you call me?'

She smiled and ran her finger round the top of her coffee cup. 'I was intrigued. The other day when we met at your dad's. I wanted to know more.'

'About what?'

'About . . . you.'

Silence. Was this really happening? Was this girl, the one who had hijacked his head, really coming on to him like this?

They talked and laughed some more.

'What's that book?'

And the laughter stopped. Sol frowned.

'Just something my old man sent me. Can you believe it? Look at the state of it.'

She took it from him and let it fall open. The book looked so much bigger in her small, gentle hands. She handled it as if it was precious metal.

'You should treasure this,' she said.

He laughed into his mocha. 'Oh yeah, 'cause it clearly cost a lot.'

'It doesn't matter what it cost. Look at it. It's got history. And wisdom. History outside, wisdom inside. I've got an old book exactly like . . . Wait a minute – this is my book. Your dad sent it? I must have . . .' She smiled, that same smile spreading from her mouth all the way to her green and blue eyes. 'I must have left it at the studio.' She pressed it to herself then handed it to him. 'You keep it, it's packed with goodness.'

He frowned and she could see he didn't appreciate the gift: he was cool and good-looking but not the most reflective mirror in the arcade. He had the nous to crack any logic problem you served up, but seeing good sense? Like most blokes he had a blind spot the size of China. He ate all the wrong foods, and avoided the best advice. It was clearly a control thing. Attractive, hip sons of million-selling record producers didn't bother with the mundane side of life.

'Can't you see?' she said.

'I can see you.'

She shook her head and sighed. 'There's so much truth about life in here.' She rapped her knuckles against the cover of the book.

'How d'you know?' he said.

'I told you – it's my book. I love it. I know this book. Believe me – it's gold dust.'

'Truth isn't in a book, it's how you live. You can write all the wonderful ideas in the world but it's just dreaming. Truth is reality and reality is what you see every day in front of your face.'

'Love.'

'What?'

'Love. Can you see love?'

'Oh, here we go, I've heard this one before.'

'All right then. Heroes and villains – why do all stories have those?'

He shrugged. 'Because it's a useful dramatic device.'

'But from where? It must come from somewhere. This idea of good over evil. Personality, quirks, diversity, hope. It all comes from somewhere.'

'Genes,' he said. 'DNA. Mother Nature. Father Time.'

'There's more to life than just substance, Sol. There's a story behind the story.'

'Very profound. Want another coffee?'

'Why are you mad with me?'

'I'm not mad with you. It's just that . . . you people, you . . . you're such control freaks. You wanna control everyone. You can't dominate the world. You can't. You can't persuade me over to your way of thinking. You're too small. Just live and let live. Lie back a little. Let the world turn without trying to give it an extra push.'

Abby nodded and connected for a second with him, her eyes locking on his, but then she pulled away, and never made eye contact again during the rest of the conversation. They sat in silence for a while. Then she slid a DVD case across the table.

'There you go, big boy. Watch that and melt a little.'

'I take it this is the best movie in the world?'

She smiled and nodded. He took it and flipped open the case. Trevor Howard and Celia Johnson clutched each other in a plume of smoke. 'The best movie in the world' was scrawled across their faces.

'See?' She tapped the disc and the scribbled words with a long fingernail. 'That proves it.'

'Nice handwriting.'

She grinned. 'Watch it,' she said.

'I already have. I've got a copy.'

'Yeah, but this isn't any old version. This is my version, this is the deluxe version.'

'I bet they still don't get together,' said Sol.

'Watch it and see,' said Abby.

'I know someone who should,' he said.

She cocked an eyebrow, in just the way the landlady had done in the doorway of her pub. 'One of your many conquests?'

Sol shook his head. 'No, just . . . just a . . . brief encounter. Hey – I'm thinking of travelling,' he said, 'doing the world on a motorbike. That or kill myself. Wanna come?'

'On which ride? The world or suicide?'

He grinned. 'I think you can work that out, but talking of riding . . .' And it was his turn to raise a single eyebrow. It was wasted on her; she was losing interest in him.

When Sol left the coffee shop five long minutes later, they didn't say a proper goodbye and he wasn't in the best of moods, which was probably why he forgot the book and the film and left them both in a circle of mocha on the table.

He went back later but Abby and the book had gone, and so had Trevor and Celia.

Running free

It was Cain's final morning at home, though when he woke he didn't know it. The last time he'd wake up in that old house. The last time he'd lie in bed staring up at those cobwebbed corners and that Dr Who lampshade. The one with Tom Baker all over it.

It wasn't meant to be the last day; it wasn't planned; it was just supposed to be another morning. Cain and his dad were too much alike, the chip had too much in common with the block. He'd never forget that final few hours. It wasn't meant to be goodbye, but the fuse had been burning for a while, and on that day there was little of it left. When Cain sauntered up the path, Adam was doing what he always did with his free time: hiding out at his allotment, avoiding his wife and stewing over his past. The guy had shocking white hair, a bristling square chin and sunlashed saddlebag skin. As he pummelled the hard ground with his creosote-spattered spade, he looked for all the world like a cross between Desperate Dan and Father Christmas.

'What's up, lad?' he asked, without looking up.

'It's Abby. I hate her.'

'Don't be stupid, you're eighteen, not five. All brothers and sisters fight. What is it this time?'

How could he say? Where could he begin? How could he disclose the obvious fact that his parents were the cause? That they treated her like a movie star and him like a scumbag, as if Cain was something unfortunate his dad was scraping off his spade and smearing on his rhubarb.

'You don't treat us the same.'

'What?' His dad looked up and there was that usual little sneer playing at the right corner of his mouth. That sneer never really left his face, sometimes it hid, but it was always there lurking in the shadows, playing behind his eyes, ever ready to be unleashed on him, or his mother. But never on Abby.

'What happened to you, Dad?'

'What do you mean?'

'Before I was born. You didn't live round here.'

Adam went back to his digging; it was a good distraction technique. He bent and flicked the earth from the corner of a jagged rock, embedded deep in the soil. There were days when Cain's dad looked a hundred years old. 'Times change,' he said.

'Was it your fault or Mum's?'

Adam looked up and stared. No sneer evident now. 'Was what my fault?'

Cain looked off into the distance. The allotments were empty apart from one or two other diggers and scrapers.

'I came across a newspaper article . . . on the net. A couple of write-ups actually. Your name came up. Some dark doings up north. Some . . . indiscretion. Helping yourself to stuff that was out of your reach.'

Adam's weathered skin took on an auburn hue. Was it anger or embarrassment?

'It's gone. It's past.'

'But it isn't, is it? It lives on. In you, in Mum, in the silences, in the way you treat me 'cause I'm too much like you . . .'

The slap wasn't expected. It shut Cain up and left a stinging smear across his cheek. His dad raised his hand to strike a second time.

'When I was your age we had some respect,' he said through gritted teeth.

'No, Dad, I don't think you did. I think you like to think so. But clearly you crossed lines and took liberties. What was it all about? Did you go to prison? Did Mum? What the hell went on?'

Adam's hand was still in the air, poised to lash out again. Eventually he spoke. 'We had a good life, your mother and I. A perfect life. We were just stupid, couldn't see a gift horse when it was right there sniffing our shoes.'

He shut up and lowered his hand, went back to digging. He smacked the spade against the jagged rock and stopped, nursing his jolted hand. Cain waited; there was more, there had to be more.

'We ran a small company. Fruit farming. Started small and grew rapidly. It was all we'd ever wanted: nice part of the world, independence, freedom. Perfect.'

Adam looked off into the distance and screwed up his eyes, as if he could still see the place, somewhere on the horizon. The crow's-feet around his eyes deepened.

'It wasn't up north though, maybe if it had been he wouldn't have been around to trip us up. Can't even remember the guy's name now, some smooth shyster in snakeskin shoes who turned up one day with this scheme that would catapult us into the big time. So he claimed. But slimy strangers speak with a forked tongue. Your mother got tempted and . . . well, she persuaded me. I don't know why we fell for it. We had everything. We didn't need any more, didn't want a brand name or some poncy global market. But we got greedy . . . and greed paints all kinds of elusive pictures in your head.' He stared off into the distance again, squinting at his long-lost Eden. He silently muttered to himself. Cain waited. Eventually Adam shook his head and hurled the spade at the rock again. 'Haven't you got something else to be getting on with?'

Running free

'Keep talking, I'm listening . . .'

Adam shook his head. 'No, you're not. And what good is it anyway, won't bring back what we had. Won't stop your mother crying herself to sleep at night. Won't stop me wishing the days away. Once you've had everything son, you can never have it again.'

'That's stupid,' snapped Cain.

Adam turned on him again, his eyes a couple of fireballs raging in his leathery face. 'Go away before I do something that will only make things worse.'

Cain started to walk away. For a moment there his old man had seemed almost human.

'Hey,' his father called and Cain looked back, hopeful for something more. 'Where did you find the story on the internet?'

Cain shook his head, turned away and didn't glance back. 'Doesn't matter,' he muttered.

There never was a story.

Two hours later, Cain stood in his room staring at the black book in his hands. He'd found it among a heap of DVDs in his sister's room. The cover was scarred and mottled: it had obviously seen some action. The sweat was still on Cain's fingers and his prints were adding fresh marks to the leather. A few tiny flecks of red fell out from under his nails and added to the pattern. He flipped open the cover and past the first few pages, then stared at the first chapter.

A new world was kicking in right in front of his eyes. New possibilities, new people, new places. That's what he needed right now. Somewhere he could go and start again. Somewhere away from the trouble. He shut the book and dropped it into his bag along with a few of the films.

PART TWO

PART TWO

The last man on earth

Cain hated being alone. At six foot three, and with green Mohawk hair, he stood out from the crowd anyway. (Why did everyone call it a Mohican? Mohicans had long hair, it was Mohawks that had the shocked cockerel look.) He'd always been different, started sprouting legs at primary school and was head and shoulders above the crowd by the time he left aged eleven. Most people complimented him on his towering limbs and bony good looks. But Cain wasn't fooled. He knew the truth. He felt awkward and conspicuous and people picked on him – for the answers in class and fights in the playground. Life had dealt him a bad hand. Sporting the Mohawk only added to the height, of course, but people always did that, didn't they – accentuate the bits of themselves they hated, in a vain attempt to distract others.

And now he was on the run. Like the last man on earth fleeing the coming storm. He'd chucked everything he owned in the back of his ailing Skoda (another attempt to hide his height that only highlighted the problem) and he drove round and round for three days and nights, stopping in lay-bys, crumbling pubs and gloomy recreation grounds to catch some sleep here and there. He had no job but a couple of grand in the bank, accrued from a few painting and decorating jobs and a recent

~y from a dead uncle who'd always had a soft spot or his lanky wayward nephew.

So when he rolled up at Peniel Green and took one look at Renegade's Rest he knew the place was for him. At least for now. Not forever, nothing was forever.

The place was in a mess. An old run-down Georgian farmhouse, in its own rampant acre of sun-fried cow dung, and hip high nettles. No one had touched the place in years and Cain knew straight away it was for him.

Peniel Green was just a pub, a church and a few dozen houses hanging around here and there. There once had been a green, but not any more: a handful of new houses had swallowed it up with their sprawling gardens. A single street cut the little community in half, the main road to somewhere else, to life away from the yawning farmland and dozy cows.

You couldn't even get a decent mobile signal.

Which was fine for Cain as he'd tossed his Ericsson under the wheels of his car on his way out of his past life; for once grateful that you could lose the entire back catalogue of your existence simply by disposing of your phone.

Renegade's Rest was owned by Enoch Judd, an oak beam of a man with thick grey hair and a permanent crimson hue to his complexion. He'd farmed the land round those parts for decades, through thick and thin. And still farmed bits of it now, but not at Renegade's Rest. He was happy to cordon off that bit and leave it to any rookie stupid enough to want to take it on and do it up. Just pay the weekly rent and he'd be happy. It wasn't a pittance but it was laughable compared to the city. And no, he didn't do standing orders. Cash in hand, thanks.

The last man on earth

Renegade's Rest just about passed as furnished, though he'd be tempted to use most of it for fuel; there was a vast fireplace in the dark sitting room at one end of the building. The other end held a kitchen and a bathroom. The bath was as expected: an old iron tub with huge tarnished taps and a chainless plug the size of a small cowpat.

Between the kitchen and the sitting room there was a dining room containing a large oval table, chestnut drinks cabinet (crystal decanters sadly empty) and the wooden stairs up to the first floor. Up there Cain found two small bedrooms and one master bedroom with a huge four-poster bed and half a dozen odd bits of antique furniture supporting grotesque cobwebbed Toby jugs, dust-carpeted trinket boxes and a few ancient lamps. A single bookcase lined the wall behind the bed, and there wasn't a paperback in sight: every single tome was as thick and solid as a stale loaf of bread. With the appropriate mould to match.

Cain spent a lonely half-hour unpacking. A wad of crumpled clothes, jeans and T-shirts mostly, secondhand from Oxfam and the like. The odd book and a clutch of DVDs and CDs: music and movies would be his best mates for a while, he figured.

As the black night washed over the village, Cain unloaded the last few things from the boot of his car and stored them in a temporary safe place. He'd find somewhere more permanent later. It was late when he locked the door, checking the catch three times, and tapping the handle four before he felt safe.

Cain spent the first night wandering around the place from room to room. He'd always been scared of the dark and with the onset of night, on his own in a strange place, he found it remarkably difficult to settle. The place changed under cover of darkness. It produced shapes and shadows that were invisible by daylight. He was sure he saw the face of a recently dead woman in the bleak small hours. Out the back, in the ghostly moonlight and thick shadows from the oak trees, an old outhouse crouched in the gloom, waiting there with its secrets and mysteries. He glanced at it occasionally through the kitchen window, but nothing would woo him into there. Probably infested with rats and cockroaches.

He stopped regularly to check his appearance in the huge gothic mirror – his face showed signs of the stress. He had more tubs of cream than a tea shop, he applied lashings of it morning and evening but there were times when it made little difference these days. The pressure in his head was too great and the cracks were showing. Literally.

To be honest, with the stuff he shoved up his nose for rhinitis, the stuff in his eyes for his lenses, salt water to flush out his ears, the cream on his face and toothpaste in his mouth, it felt like he couldn't walk out in the morning without shoving chemicals into every orifice. His dad would turn in his grave – one day. Adam was a no-nonsense salt-of-the-earth kind of guy – 'Why d'you need all these man-made concoctions when you've got the natural stuff? Daylight and fresh air and bit of hard work.' He could hear the old man now, dishing out good advice with a rueful shake of his head and a jab at some stubborn turf with his spade.

He spent the first week tidying up and working on the walls. Half the paper in the dining room was peeling off and in some places only held up by weakening wads of Blu-Tack.

Now all Cain needed was a job. Surely some sucker would employ a no-hoper with green Mohawk hair and size fifteen feet.

Missing

Sol was famous for the size of his DVD collection. He wasn't famous for keeping them tidy. He wasn't one of these guys who kept them alphabetised with a log book documenting when he bought them and who last borrowed them. This mattered today because he was going to take *Brief Encounter* to the landlady. If he could find it. The problem was he had a mountain of cases on the carpet alongside a mountain of DVDs. And the two mountains did not correspond. He'd put off sorting this out for too long. Some crises just couldn't wait. If he was gonna snuggle up to pub-girl in front of the small screen then he needed to track down *the best movie in the world*.

The phone rang.

'Hello?'

'Sol, it's Dave.'

There it was again, the rock'n'roll father going by his first name.

'Hi, Dad. How's things in Popland?'

'Gotta problem. My girl, Abby? Not been back for a week.'

'She's probably seen the light, mate. Realised what a grizzled old toad she's shacked up with.'

'She already knew that. But I'm serious. I'm worried. She's missing, mate, I'm sure of it. Can you put the word about? Maybe do some scouting for me?'

Scouting for Abby? It would be a pleasure.

He stopped sorting his DVDs and just shoved discs in cases in a random fashion. It was a quick fix and from a distance it looked great. He'd sort 'em out properly later.

The Memphis

Across the road from Cain's cottage was The Memphis: a rambling old pub covered in creepers and broken lattice. It was all you could do to make it inside through the oddly angled door frame. Once inside it was worth it, though. The place was awash with the finest ancient ales, the sounds of the sixties crackling away on a vinyl jukebox and dark nooks for illicit exchanges and uninterrupted drinking. The locals loved it and Cain had every intention of becoming a local.

The only downside was the two Alsatians, Ammo and Jude, who roamed freely and slavered copiously. The landlady lived alone and the two savage beasts were her insurance against drunken yobs, amorous thugs and late night intruders. She was feisty, beautiful and cool. And not afraid to call a spade a spade.

'What do you want?'

'Well, a drink first off would be nice.'

She scowled. 'We don't do nice drinks here. We do good ale.'

'A good ale then.'

She started pouring.

'And a job.'

She stopped.

'You want help, don't you?' Cain said. 'The sign on the door there says you want help.'

'It's an old sign.'

She finished pouring. 'You moved in across the road?'
He nodded.
'Not got a good history, that cottage.'
'Well . . . I wanna change history.'
'Do you now? Two fifty-five.'

He handed over four coins and she didn't count them. She didn't move actually. She just studied him with narrowed chestnut eyes. He stared back and used up all his strength trying not to flinch. She had a tiny scar trailing back from her right eyebrow.

'I don't suffer fools,' she said.
'I'm not a fool.'
'You are running from something though.'
He shrugged. 'Isn't everyone?'

Slowly, painfully slowly, she shook her head. 'I'm not running from anything. You can start on Monday. Two-week trial. Ever poured pints?'

He nodded and lied. She nodded and knew it.
'Monday, then. Don't mess me about though.'

He took his pint and hid. What was he thinking? He wanted an easy life; this was like mooching at the mouth of a volcano. Hanging about at the gates of hell. One wrong move and she'd feed him to the dogs. Nice.

Three days went by. Cain spent the time working in the garden and sitting around Renegade's Rest drinking cups of strong tea. The day before he was due to start at The Memphis he sorted out his DVD collection. He flicked through them. He'd scooped them up in a hurry so wasn't sure exactly what he'd taken. As he picked up the stack one stray disc dropped out and fell at his feet. He stared at it, as it perched there wedged between his size-fifteen boots.

The job

She was waiting for him.

'You don't even know my name,' she said, 'and you're a minute late.'

Cain looked hurt. 'No way. And it's Tamar, I heard someone say. I remembered 'cause I don't know any Tamars.'

'Well you won't get to know me. So don't get your hopes up.'

That was fine by Cain. The more remote and anonymous, the better, as far as he was concerned. Monday turned out to be a good day to start. A lot of it was lugging barrels and replacing bottles after the weekend. A few locals pitched up for lunch, some retired folk and a couple of farmers. The chef was a tiny guy called Shaun who said nothing the whole day. He did smile though, twice, which was two more times than Tamar did.

As Cain stood behind the bar that evening, watching the drinkers and the darts players, he felt like the loneliest man in the world. The last man on earth. Why did he feel so disconnected? Why did everyone else appear to fit in so well? How had life passed him by like this? Out there, beyond the ale taps, there was a seething swathe of life. People laughing and small talking, making eyes at each other and deals across the tables. He couldn't reach them, he was beginning to see that now. He'd never be one of these people for whom rubbing shoulders was a way of life. If he'd ever had that trait, it was long gone now.

'You're not paid to stare.'

It was her, Tamar.

'Sorry.'

Her chestnut eyes widened. She'd caught him off guard and he'd somehow produced an unqualified apology. She almost looked embarrassed.

'Yeah, well, there's a couple of dry customers down the end.'

During a ten-minute break, Cain ambled out the back into the garden, where he sat under the tree and leafed through the delicate pages of the black book. A sudden strafe from above and the text in front of him turned grey and white. He glanced up: a rook was making off with empty bowels. The book was defaced, not unlike the couple he'd just been reading about. He wiped the page on the grass, taking off some of the thick mess.

He'd been reading the start of everything. A man and a woman got the gift of life, and a stab at a new world.

And they threw it away.

It sounded so like his parents.

'What's that?'

Cain glanced up. Tamar was standing near him by the gate into the field that constituted the back garden. The evening sun winked at him from behind her.

'Oh, you know, the good book. I picked it up when I left home. I think it's my sister's.'

'You left home? You were still with your parents? Why d'you get out?'

He shrugged. 'I was going nowhere. You can have it if you like.' And he tossed the book at her. She caught it awkwardly and turned it in her hands as if it was an unexploded bomb.

The job

'Never had much time for this,' she said.
'Me neither,' he said.

Later that night, at the end of the shift, when she'd thrown them all out, Cain included, he wandered across the road in the moonlight and stood in the doorway of Renegade's Rest, his shoulder wedged against the rotting frame. It was never gonna work, was it? He'd changed his life but was still stuck with himself. Where could he go to get away from Cain? Nowhere. There was nowhere he'd be that Cain wouldn't be too. It was like trying to shake off your shadow.

He stayed out there until he was chilled to the bone. Then he went inside, collapsed on the huge bed and fell asleep thinking about Tamar.

Across the street Tamar poured herself a gin, switched off the lights and limped towards the stairs. The dogs were already dozing and showed little interest as she passed them in the kitchen. Upstairs, she threw her clothes across a chair and crawled under the sheet.

She'd been limping towards the end of a novel that had finally kicked into life. After two-hundred pages of character development and small print, she suddenly rounded the bend into a home strait littered with menace, sex and violence. Like waiting all month for a drink and then being offered a triple vodka. An appalling chapter of threatened rape transported her back to a short story she'd read when she was ten, and the horror of discovering that certain things existed in the world. The account came at her like a sudden overhanging branch cracking her across the face. Now, as then, she found herself attracted and repelled by what she was reading and the experience was heady, nauseous and destabilising.

It brought up other things too, later things: boys making promises and men making commitments that were little more than an excuse for their own inadequate fumblings. Once the fumbling was over so was she, history, dumped, men getting their own way. By force and bargaining. Up to this point in the book she'd been skipping pages because they were too dull, now she was skipping them because they were too potent. She couldn't face another chapter of it. Instead she flipped open Cain's black leather book and found herself reading about a beautiful woman alone without a lover. The poor girl lay in her bed and wished for him but he didn't come. And he was never gonna turn up. Been there darling, Tamar thought. In the end the madness drove the poor woman to roaming the streets in the dark, and that in turn led her into prostitution. She ended up nothing but used and abused. Tamar threw down the book in disgust. It collided with the gin glass and sent it spinning to the floor. Tamar didn't care. You weren't supposed to find that kind of stuff in the good book. It was supposed to be sweetness and light. She threw herself back on her bed and wondered what it was like to be a prostitute.

The next day

'I'm leaving.'

She looked up, startled. It was Cain, and he was late.

'Don't creep up on me like that,' she said.

'Sorry. I'm leaving.'

'Leaving where?'

'The job.'

She snorted and shut the black book. 'You're not mate, you're working the next fortnight. That's the deal.'

'I can't.'

'You have to, it's gonna be busy. I'm relying on you.'

'Don't be stupid, I've only done two days.'

'You'll be fine, anyway I'm not going anywhere, I'll be right here to wipe your nose and clear up your mess.'

'Tamar, I can't, I really can't.'

She looked at him and raised an eyebrow, the one above the tiny scar. 'You're a loser, Cain. I knew it the moment you walked in.'

'I'm not.'

'Then prove it. I always knew you were running away from something. Stands out a mile.'

'I'm not.'

'Then prove it. Don't run from this.'

'I don't like it.'

'I haven't liked it for ten years, but you get on with it.'

He stared into the middle distance. She put the book on the shelf behind her and needlessly rearranged pint glasses. There was something in the air between them. He had no idea what.

'What did you do before this?'

'I was trying to get into advertising. Had a great job lined up. It was right there waiting for me.'

'So what are you doing pulling pints?'

'It got stolen from me, things happened, things out of my control.' Cain spat the words out. He felt every one of them as they left his mouth.

'It's not the first time. I . . . I find it hard to stick at things. I get restless, I need change.' His face turned to stone. 'Right now, I feel like I'll never succeed at anything.'

She nodded, her brow furrowed, the dark lines on her forehead closing in on her eyes. 'At The Moody Cow they're doing better than us,' she said.

'What?'

'The Moody Cow up the road at Timnah. Car park's always full. That's why I need your help. Any support is good support right now. I need you, Cain. Don't run.'

Odd. She seemed suddenly vulnerable, desperate even, not the sassy woman he thought she was at all.

Her mobile rang. She raised a commanding finger to Cain and answered it.

'How did you get my number? What d'you want? . . . What? The signal's not good here. What? You got a copy of what? Oh that! You're not still going on about that old film? Forget it. I know, I remember – the station and the lovers who never get it on. It won't change anything. OK, bring it over if you have to. When? When? Oh, all right. Come any time. But don't expect anything else.'

The garden at Renegade's Rest was still a mess. It was little more than a field with a few apple trees and a strawberry patch thrown in for good measure. So the

The next day

next afternoon, on his day off, Cain took an excursion into extreme horticulture: hacking at wild, thigh-high grass with an old sickle that he found rusting away outside the kitchen, beside an ancient crud-encrusted water pump. The thing had been half covered in lichen and strangling ivy. He wrestled it free, ripped off the wild green barbed wire and laid into the undergrowth. There was a certain satisfaction in being violent. Weeds didn't bleed, or scream for mercy. As the afternoon wore on and the sky melted exquisitely into a rosy hue of sunset, he stood surrounded by dying stinging nettles and clumps of butchered grass, pondering the tattered remnants of his life. He wiped the sweat from his grass-flecked brow and stared longingly into the dying of the light. Another glorious death of another summer's day; this show was a regular in this neck of the woods. Maybe it was a sign, maybe it would be OK after all, maybe this really was the beginning of the rest of his life.

Brief encounter

Sol had started out well enough. He was intelligent, attractive and athletic. But not popular: there was just something too self-assured, too gleaming, too eager about this rock child. His mates fawned at first, but most of them saw through the shining exterior and the well-rehearsed presentation. Sol was flawed, however shiny his smile. And multiple women were just about his biggest flaw. One look at Abby had begun a rapid spiral into obsession, while the brief encounter with Tamar had fuelled an overpowering desire to subdue her wild spirit and wrestle it to the ground. Literally. He spent some time putting the word out about Abby, but no one seemed to know much about her. So he went after the other woman instead and found himself braving his backside and calves, standing on the doorstep of The Memphis, with the sound of the Alsatians snapping in the background.

Tamar came to the door looking tired and stressed. She took the movie from him with little acknowledgement and closed the door. The only consolation was her invitation for him to return for it in a couple of days.

Tamar held out the DVD case. Trevor Howard and Celia Johnson looked deep into each other's eyes. They'd never have each other, but their longing would last forever.

'I didn't watch it,' she said, surly as ever.

Sol frowned. 'Why not, you tart? It's a classic.'

'Don't call me that – I know you're joking but don't. It's not in there.'

'What?'

'The movie's not in there. It's the wrong one. You should be more tidy. Want a drink before you go?'

'I was thinking I might not go.'

She narrowed her chestnut eyes, folded her arms protectively and studied him. The silence was unnerving.

'I'll . . . just have the drink then,' he said cautiously.

She nodded and poured him a whisky. A large one. A huge one. Maybe his luck was in after all.

'I got a new guy working here, some strange kid who's just moved in across the street. You couldn't check him out for me, could you?'

'Why?' Sol flipped open the DVD case and stared at Leonardo DiCaprio. 'This isn't *Brief Encounter*,' he said.

'I told you that. It's *The Beach*: that's why I didn't watch it. I hate DiCaprio. Give me a man over that boy any day.' She fixed him again with her narrowed eyes.

'*The Beach* is all right,' he said. 'But I have to find *Brief Encounter*. I want to lend it to you.'

'Not my problem,' she said. 'Organise your DVDs. Now, will you do it?'

'Do what?'

'Clock that punk across the road for me. I don't trust him.'

'So why did you hire him?'

She paused and ran a finger down her neck and slowly traced the neckline of her shirt. 'I like living dangerously.'

He felt intimidated now, like he was one of her dogs on some retractable lead.

'Who's got *Brief Encounter* then?' he muttered. 'You're sure it wasn't in here?'

'What you worried about some stupid film for?'

He forced a smile. 'No film is stupid, any piece of dross can have a moment of truth glistening in the celluloid excrement.'

'Yeah, yeah, Mr Ross.'

He shut the case and shook his head. 'I need to find *Brief Encounter* and, knowing the state of my DVD collection, if I'm not careful it'll be like that damn googlewhacking thing. My track record's not good. It could send me on some wild goose chase. I'll be turning into Dave Gorman.'

Her mouth morphed into a sinister smile. 'Well, Mr Gorman, how about googlewhacking me?'

Sol downed his whisky. Not quite in one, he wasn't man enough for that: the corrosive stuff burnt a track in his throat and he had to come up for air. She watched him and didn't take her eyes off him as she sipped Southern Comfort. She ran the tip of her tongue across her top lip and waited.

Sol tried to clear his throat. It wasn't easy.

'Well?' she said again.

He raised a hand, stumbled to the sink, flushed water into his glass and washed his throat with it.

'Why not?' he said eventually, his voice rasping as he spoke.

She grinned, took his glass and refilled it.

'Come up in five minutes,' she said, 'and I expect you to show me what Celia Johnson was missing.'

Standing in the dark in the abandoned bar, Sol got the usual rush of adrenalin. How many was this now in the last week? Four? Five? However you counted and however many it was, he still got his hopes up, still believed that one day he'd find the perfect girl. It was unlikely to be Tamar: she'd clearly been round the block too many times: too hard, too cynical. Wouldn't know romance if it stepped off a train and wooed her on a railway station.

But it was worth a try. There was always a chance, always the possibility this connection would be the one.

Later, much later, when it was over, and they'd both satisfied and proved themselves, Sol sat up in bed and turned the black book in his hands. He'd seen this before.

'How did you get this?'

Tamar lay still with her eyes shut against the invasive moonlight. 'You can take it if you want,' she said eventually.

'There's a missing girl – friend of my old man's – I last saw this in her hands.'

'Well, you should try the dude across the road at Renegade's – he gave it to me.'

Before driving home the following day Sol crossed the street and knocked on the cottage door. The place was as quiet and anonymous as an unmarked grave, but Sol kept on knocking and eventually a lanky guy with a Mohawk haircut came to the door.

'Yep?'

'The landlady at The Memphis told me you gave her this?' He held up the stained book.

The guy nodded.

'How did you get it?'

'It's my sister's.'

'Where did she get it?' Sol asked.

He shrugged. 'She likes that kind of stuff.'

'Can you ask her for me?' He held up a card. 'She can email me on this address. I'd appreciate it. It's important.'

The guy took the card and squinted at it. 'Why should I give her some strange bloke's email?'

'Because whoever gave her that book got it from a missing girl.'

'I'll tell her,' he said.

'D'you want to give this back to her?' asked Sol.

He shook his head. 'I gave it to Tamar.'

Sol weighed the book in his hands and nodded slowly. 'I'll get it back to her then,' he said.

He didn't. He took it home.

Dinah

He met Dinah in a bar in the city the next night. They were both on the hunt for emergency sex so it suited everyone just fine. She was a five foot brunette with curves in all the right places. And some in the wrong places too. He launched his favourite chat-up lines on her ('That dress is fantastic, it would look great in a crumpled pile on my bedroom carpet') then took her home along with Tamar's book and they had a pick-up sandwich – supper and breakfast, with sex in the middle.

The next morning they lounged around for a while.

Dinah padded across the carpet and leant on the window ledge. Something caught her eye. 'Are those allotments?'

Sol sauntered in with a double mocha the size of Waterloo Station in his hands. 'Here.'

She glanced down at the vat of caffeine.

'Do you have an allotment? You can really make something of those things. Good soil round here, you know.'

'Look, Michaela Strachan, I have better things to do than shovel the rejected contents of a cow's bowels.'

She looked at him and blinked twice. 'There's nothing better to do in the entire world than shovel bovine bowel movements.'

Maybe she wasn't the girl for him after all. There were moments last night when he had thought she might be.

She was beautiful and funny and passionate, and they laughed a lot and seemed to agree on more things than he expected. He'd even disclosed his secret plans about building a massive new complex dedicated to his dad and his beloved Radio Therapy Records. He didn't tell many people about that kind of stuff.

'You've got a lot of movies,' she said, drifting over to the shelf and thumbing through the cases.

'I wrote you a poem,' he said, but she barely seemed to notice.

'Ah! You've got *The Beach*. I love *The Beach*. I wouldn't mind a date sandwich with Leo sometime. I just read the book actually. Oh!'

'What?'

She was staring at the inside of the case. 'It's not the movie.'

'Which movie?'

'*The Beach*. It has something else in it. That thing with Denzel Washington in.' She peered at it. '*Trading Day*.'

'*Training Day*!'

'That's it.' She held it up and showed him.

He snapped his fingers and ran to the DVD stack. He hooked out the case for *Training Day* and pulled it open. 'Damn.'

'What is it?'

'It's *The Commitments*. I want it to be *Brief Encounter*.'

'I saw the case for *The Commitments* over there.' She leant over and pulled out a second case. That contained *Went the Day Well*? The case for that held *When Harry Met Sally* which in turn contained *Black Hawk Down*.

'Don't you put anything back in the right cases? I could never marry you.'

'I wasn't offering.'

The case for *Black Hawk Down* wasn't there.

'Never mind, tell me about the poem. The one you wrote for me.'

'Oh, you were listening then.' He smiled coyly and pulled a sheaf of papers from his back pocket.

'Grief. It's like *Lord of the Rings*,' she said.

He snapped his fingers at her. She flinched.

'Bingo. My old man. I lent him *Black Hawk Down* and *Gladiator*. Except it wasn't *Gladiator* in the case, it was *Lord of the Rings*.' He shoved the pages at her and picked up his phone. He dialled and waited.

'Dad, did I lend you *Black Hawk Down*? Go check the case, will you? Go. It's important. And that reminds me. Any news of Abby?'

Sol threw a guilty glance at Dinah as he said this, but she was engrossed in the poem. She was smiling. A very big smile indeed.

'No, sorry Dad, I've found nothing yet. I haven't started looking properly, really. But I will. I'll try and put the word round. What? You got it? What's in the case? *Heaven's Above*? That old Peter Seller's number? Right, OK. Cheers.'

Dinah stood up and walked towards him. 'This is about me? You wrote this for me?'

He was going to say, 'Yeah, I got up early,' but he couldn't. She kissed him hard and pulled him onto the sofa.

Dinah worked in a record store, one that Leah often visited.

On a quiet day Dinah took in a good book and read a couple of hundred pages. She read fast. She loved most things, but especially anything that featured sex and travel. She'd just finished *Girl with a One-track Mind*. She kept a blog too, and an allotment. When she wasn't reading, watching or blogging she was out in the real world. Shovelling bovine bowel movements.

'I'm worried about a mate of mine,' Dinah said.

'Hmm?' Leah was in, taking a break from busking and thumbing through some old Joni Mitchell discs.

'Abby. She's gone missing.'

'Never met her,' said Leah with a yawn. 'Where's she hang out?'

'I only know her from the allotments. She has the one next to mine.'

Leah put the discs down and scowled. 'Dinah, I just can't see you with a shovel in your hand, girl.'

'Give me a man or a shovel, I know what to do with either. Actually, came across a good one last night.'

'Shovel?'

'Man. Funny name. Sol, he was called.'

'I know a Sol,' said Leah. 'Well, I don't but Jake does. He's in the music business.'

Dinah's face lit up. 'You're kidding me. Tall? Good-looking? Full of himself?'

'That doesn't narrow it down much.' Leah sauntered over, pushing her guitar around and out of the way so it hung down her back. 'So, you gonna see him again?'

Dinah raised an eyebrow and tapped the page she was reading. 'He was hot,' she said, 'and he let me borrow a few movies and books.'

'Oh well, when you moving in?'

'He's got a gorgeous flat. Money money money in the family.'

Leah reached over and picked up the black book. 'This isn't your usual pulp fiction, girl.'

'It's hard going actually. And I just started something else. You might find some good song ideas in there though. Perfect for you Tracey Chapman fans. All gloom and doom.'

Leah stared at the page. Something had caught her eye.

'Borrow it if you like,' said Dinah. 'Hello, you all right there? Can I help you?'

'Do you have the Wurzels' Greatest Hits?'

Leah turned and eyed the ten year old. 'I don't think they ever had any,' she said, and with a forced grin she shut the black leather book and went outside.

'Dinah, it's me, Sol.'

Dinah raised her eyebrows and smiled into the phone. There was no one else there to see it, as the store was empty.

'Hi, gorgeous,' she said.

'Dinah.' He sounded businesslike, brisk: not in the mood for telephonic foreplay.

'Dinah, do you know someone called Abby? Abby Mann?'

'I was just talking about her. She's gone missing.'

'So I hear.'

'How d'you know her, Sol?'

A pause on the other end of the line. Dinah did the emotional maths in her head. 'Don't worry,' she said. 'I get the picture.'

'Actually she's my dad's girlfriend. You don't have her address, do you?'

'I know she's from over Eden way. Her old man's a fierce old bear.'

'Got his number?'

'No, but I know they live on a redundant farm there. Been turned into a load of old allotments. Her parents hired the land out after things went sour for them.'

Over Eden way

Adam was stooped over a forkful of dung when Sol approached the gate. The wood was rotting and the catch broken and useless.

'Mr Mann? Are you Adam Mann?'

Adam looked up, his weathered face hardening as Sol smiled at him.

'You hadn't better have come to tell me she's in a ditch somewhere,' he growled and flecks of silver spit followed the words out of his mouth. 'She's everything to me, everything. First I lose her mother, now her. Haven't seen Cain in days either.' He shook his head and continued talking to himself, as he spaded the ground and jammed manure between the hard clumps of earth.

'Her mother's missing too?' Sol asked, leaning on the gate gingerly.

'Might as well be, we haven't had a decent conversation in years. What do you want? Do you know where Abby is?'

Sol pulled out his silver hip flask and offered it to the white-haired old man. Adam shrugged and strolled over, walking bow-legged as if he'd just ridden hard for three days.

'Alcohol won't loosen my tongue,' he muttered as he unscrewed the cap.

'When did you last see Abby?' Sol asked gently.

The old man tipped the flask and shrugged. He wiped his mouth. 'Few days back,' he said. 'But she never stays away like this. I know something's happened. Probably that Svengali boyfriend of hers, twisted old rock star, bet he's pumped her with drugs and sold her into slavery. Bastard.'

Sol smiled. 'I doubt it.'

'Why you looking for her anyway?' Adam narrowed his eyes as he spoke. 'Are you police?'

'Just a friend.' He proffered a business card; it was reassuringly expensive. 'Have you told the cops then?'

'Of course. Take no notice though. You have to be missing a decade before the Bill show any interest. Listen, if you do find anything – you will tell me, won't you? As bad as it may be, I can't live with not knowing. I just want her back.' The old man's eyes welled up: he wasn't as tough as his skin made out.

Sol nodded and took a swig of his flask.

The old man sniffed and snorted back the tears. 'Life wasn't supposed to be like this,' he barked. 'All work and sweat and heartbreak. It was supposed to be laughter, and family, and doing stuff together.'

Sol nodded. 'Can I speak to your wife?' he asked.

'Eve's back at the farmhouse, blaming me for losing her kids. Seth's at home too.' His eyes brightened. 'Seth's a good lad, the only thing that keeps us together really.'

Sol put away his flask, smiled at Adam and went. He walked over to the farmhouse, a chipped yellowing building, covered in bindweed and moss; the roof was missing tiles and a few of the window panes were bunged up with rags and cardboard. The whole place stank of regret. A young guy in his late teens came out to meet him; it was the first smile Sol had seen in a while. He looked somehow familiar.

'Have we met before?' Sol asked, taking the boy's outstretched hand.

'Doubt it,' said Seth, 'Cuppa tea? Dad phoned ahead, said you were wandering round looking for us. Have you seen Abby or Cain?'

Sol snapped his fingers. 'Cain,' he said. 'Cain.'

'Yup, my brother, can't miss him, eight foot tall and a head like a cockerel.'

'Yeah, I think I met him – he looks like you.'

Seth raised a pierced eyebrow and said, 'Thanks a lot!'

He took Sol inside. A woman in her fifties was sitting on an old leather sofa at one end of the huge kitchen, staring at daytime television. She stood up as Sol came in. She was short and slim and her greying hair was tied back in a ponytail. She wore no make-up and her face had the same hard look as her husband's, as if they'd both lived through too many disappointments.

Sol spotted Abby in her eyes though. There was no mistaking that.

'Mum, this is Sol. He's trying to find Abby for you.'

'Well, not entirely just for you, but someone's asked me to see what's going on.'

She shook her head and smiled. 'I hope you have some luck,' she said, 'goodness knows we need it.'

Seth showed his mother Sol's business card.

'Not exactly a private detective, are you?' she said.

Sol shook his head. 'I was wondering, I know it's an intrusion, but can I see her room?'

Trevor and Celia were the first thing Sol spotted.

'Great movie,' he said to Seth who had followed him in.

'I'm more of a Bruce Willis guy myself,' said Seth.

'I guess she'd have a copy, eh? Only I promised I'd lend someone this movie. A friend of mine's never seen it.'

'Oh yeah, she has a copy all right, the mega-deluxe, double-stiff-upper-lip, all-singing-all-dancing, extra-fries version. She's made me watch it a million times.'

Seth crouched down beside a small stack of movies. He quickly thumbed through. 'Here we go – oh! No, that's not it. Oh. Odd, it's not here. Should be right there, Abby's organised about these things. Can't believe it. No copy of *Brief Encounter*.'

Angels in the graveyard

Leah picked up the black book and thumbed the scarred pages. This thing had seen some action. Two of the pages were glued together by something very nasty. She lay back in the massive bath and rested the book on her soap-caked knees. She let her eyes wander round the huge bathroom. The black and grey wall tiles, the gleaming chrome, the classic juke box in the far corner, the massive shower cubicle the size of three telephone boxes and big enough for all the Rolling Stones to use in one go. In fact, so Jake claimed, Mick Jagger had once taken a shower in it. But that thought just made Leah shudder: he may have been a god in the sixties but now he held all the appeal of a wrinkled goblin. Glancing round at his designer bathroom the question occurred to her yet again, how could a DJ of Jake's standing finance this? The whole chapel had been trashed and reborn under Jake's watchful eye. Only the pulpit and a few of the pews still remained, the pulpit looming large like the Eiffel Tower, smack in the middle of Jake's designer lounge, facing the colossal wall-mounted TV. A ragged Bart Simpson stood in it at present, peeking over the top, stuffed and ready to preach. Oh, and there were also the other remnants, one or two of them even in here, little stone epitaphs to the long gone – a reminder, said Jake, that 'in the midst of life, we're in death' (or in Leah's case, 'debt'). She stared at one of the epitaphs now, right ahead of her at eye level, Nimrod Cush, died nearly a century ago, in a good cause, on a foreign field, for an empire long gone. Climbing out of a trench strewn with filth and body parts, where men lived with rats and lice and abandoned their sanity. She frowned and dragged her eyes back to the black book again. It was hard to read. The room was stifling, the bathwater stinging her skin, steam pawing at her face and clawing at her eyes, and relentless lines of water dripping from her hair down her nose. It was inevitable, really. Sooner or later she was going to drop the book in the bath.

It was sooner. She was just adjusting her position when the damp bundle slipped off her knees and splashed beneath the water. Fishing it out was no mean achievement.

Leah was freaked the first time Jake brought her home. She'd never met anyone who lived in a church in the middle of a graveyard. The place was full of leering gothic faces and whispering voices from the past. She half expected to wake up and find his teeth in her neck. Jake clearly loved the place and at some point on most days he found time to sit on the rock just outside the porch, right beneath the scowling cherub, watching the mist shimmer in the trees, stroking the tombstones as it went by.

'I once saw a load of angels in this graveyard,' he told her that first evening as he sat outside and she skulked in the porch.

'And you're still living here?'

He laughed. 'I was on the run, I'd only slipped in here to get some kip. It was a real misty night, could barely see the graveyard out there.'

'Well, I s'pose that's some consolation.'

'Listen, will you? I was half asleep and I heard these footsteps and over there, resting against that oak tree, just beyond the big marble cross ... See it? Well, there was this massive silver ladder rising up out of the fog, and then I saw this huge gleaming figure seep upwards out of the ground, like the night of the living dead or something, and then another one got up and another one, and they all started climbing the ladder, going up and then back down it. Like they were on a divine escalator.'

'How much had you had to drink exactly?'

Jake ignored her, stood up and started towards the oak tree. 'You'd think I'd have been spooked right? No way. I did this, I went over, towards the shining figures and when I looked up I saw ...'

He stopped and shivered then.

'I thought you said it didn't spook you?'

'It didn't. It just does now.'

She waited for him to finish but he simply stood there, gazing up into the black sky. She wandered over and stumbled between the stones, scraping her legs as she went.

'You could sell up and buy a nice little cottage somewhere. One without all the dead people.'

'No I couldn't, 'cause I met him here. He was up there.' And he shivered again.

'Who? Frankenstein?'

'No. God.' He said it so straightforwardly, as if he hadn't just said the most ridiculous thing in the world. 'The funny thing is,' he continued, and he shivered again, 'at the time it was amazing ... and that's why I bought the place. But now – I just feel guilty, like I ran away from the experience 'cause I couldn't live up to it.' He looked at her and gave an innocent smile. 'I'm not religious you know.'

'Sure, you just live in a church and talk to angels in a graveyard. Come on, I need a Bacardi.'

And she'd gone inside, leaving him staring up into the night sky, surrounded by his ghostly memories and a hundred corpses. Nutter.

Angels in the graveyard

He was out there again this evening. Espresso cupped in his hands, steam rising and mingling with the night mist. Somewhere in the distance the moor sheep and goats were coughing and bleating. She went out and sat on his rock, still wrapped in her bathrobe, little droplets of water still sitting on her arms and neck.

'See any angels?' she yelled.

Jake shook his head and supped his coffee. 'Doubt if I'll bump into any more of them,' he said. 'Hey! We could have supper outside.'

'No, we couldn't.'

He came over and took the sodden book from her wet hands. It had swelled to twice its size and the fluid dripping from it was a brown mixture of soap, coffee, beer and bird mess.

'Find anything useful in your book of wisdom there?'

She didn't answer; the thing was in soggy disarray, the pages bulging with honey and jasmine bathwater.

'D'you pray, Jake?' She took the mug from him and clutched it to herself, in the vain hope that the steaming warmth might permeate her whole body.

'What?' he said.

'D'you say prayers? I mean you're always on about God and angels and gravestones. And you live in a church . . .'

'I'm not always going on about God . . .'

'And why are you out here looking up at that tree again? Waiting for another ladder?'

He sighed and clutched his jumper round him; it was way too big now, stretched from years of tearing it on and off. 'I don't know. I used to pray. No, I still do. But not 'cause I'm religious – it's like a default thing. I daren't not pray. When I'm stressed or panicked I just spout the things.'

'That sounds like superstition.'

'You asked.'

'I don't get it though, and there's no sugar in this coffee. You say you believe in God and all that but you don't pray.'

'I just said I do pray! You're not listening. What I mean is I don't understand it, I'm not sure why I do it, but I do. OK? No more clues. End of story.'

'My sister prays. She prays all the time, that and talking to herself. In fact, I think she's not able to work out which is which. The talking and praying. She reckons people are the face of God, making the . . . what is it? . . . visible invisible. She should be a woman priest.'

'Look, now you've drunk my coffee and ruined my space out here – why don't we just have sex?'

'That's your answer to everything isn't it?'

'Why not?'

''Cause for you it solves everything, for me it solves nothing.'

'I don't know, that's not quite the way you expressed it last night . . .'

They went and had sex.

And he did his best not to think of Rach.

Circular rock'n'roll

'Back in the fifties Deano Max founded So-so Records. So-so's biggest artist was Mindy Meek. Mindy's first husband ran off with Katie Late who at the time was signed to Plant Pot Records. Plant Pot was owned by Killer Kind and Killer was cousin to Sweet Louise Slowhand who played bass for the Hankie Pankies. The Hanky Pankies' first hit was called "Don't Go Pulling My Leg" and "Don't Go Pulling My Leg" spent fifteen weeks at the top of the chart and was a worldwide smash. Well, "Don't Go Pulling" was co-written by fifteen-year-old Sammy Brash and Sammy's uncle was engaged for six months to Carol Yak who was bridesmaid to Julia Jackass. Julia married none other than Snake Madd and Snake Madd had set up Sneak Thief Studios with Hoosier Dang and Cute Curly Brown, and Cute Curly was, believe it or not, Deano Max's chiropractor. And as we've already established Deano Max founded So-so Records. So average punters, how's that for a circular rock'n'roll story? Another one coming your way tomorrow. Anyway, here's the Saws with "African Cow Herdsman".'

Jake didn't know how much of these tales were true, he got a lot of them from an old schoolmate who got them from his dad who swore blind that every word was solid gold, every full stop set in concrete. He'd just picked this one up this morning, found it among a stash of emails that had not been checked for a week. And that's what gave him the idea. He'd had the dad on the show; why not get the son on? And make good use of him while he was in the studio.

'Leah.'

She looked reluctantly towards him with her stunning blue eyes. As if it was hard and detestable work to switch her gaze from her magazine to him.

'I might be able to get you a recording contract. Would you want that?'

She sat up in bed like a shot. 'Er . . . no, I think I'd rather spend the rest of my life singing in the gutter. Course I would. What are you talking about? How come you suddenly thought of this?'

'I got an old friend, don't really know him well, he just sends me stuff for the radio, stories and trivia and stuff. Tonight I found a great one about . . .'

'Jake. Focus. I don't give a splashback about his stories. Cut to the chase.'

Jake sighed and stared up at the ceiling. He couldn't help thinking Rach would have loved the story about Deano Max and the Hankie Pankies. Such great names. Such simple tuneful times. He sighed and cut to the chase. 'He's a talent scout for his old man. His dad's one of the big names in the business. I interviewed him recently. I reckon I could invite the guy on the show and maybe if you came on too and sang live . . .'

'Nathan, it's Sol, did I lend you *Heaven's Above*? Can you check the case? Go on, I'll wait . . . What? *A Beautiful Mind*. Thanks.'

'Shim, did you take *A Beautiful Mind* the other day? I know, it's the wrong case isn't it? What's in there then? *Music & Lyrics*. I'd forgotten I had that. Thanks.'

'Ellie – d'you have *Music and Lyrics*? Yeah? So what's actually in there? *Hannibal*? Oops sorry. Yeah I know I really need to organise 'em all. I'm sorry, I'll do better next time. *Hitch*? Yeah I got that – somewhere. D'you wanna borrow it? I can't see it right at this moment but I'm sure I had it. Yeah, mind you, it probably contains *Psycho* – but you can still borrow it. Ellie? Ellie?'

Romeo's baby

Jake stuck his head in from outside and grabbed his espresso. Leah was cooking up a storm for supper. There were abandoned saucepans everywhere: it looked like the kitchen equivalent of Dunkirk.

'This version of "Romeo and Juliet" is awesome,' he said, nodding sagely.

'Is it?' she forced a grin. There was mushroom sauce on the bridge of her nose.

'Yeah. Can't you hear?'

'Sounds better than Status Quo,' she said.

'It wasn't Status Quo. Status Quo didn't do the original, they could never do this.'

'Well, Queen then.'

'Queen? Queen! Does it sound like a Freddy Mercury number?

'I don't listen to Freddy Mercury. I prefer Mika.'

'It was Dire Straits and it's a classic. I thought you were into music.'

'I am. Just not like you.' She abandoned another saucepan and grabbed two more. The clatter drowned out the next part of the song.

'You always say that,' he said when musical order had been resumed.

'You always say stupid things about old songs – there's more to life you know.'

'What like make-up and magazines and the latest jeans?'

'What's that mean?'

Jake was in it for the music – he might have had unfathomable taste but he believed in that unfathomable taste. He wasn't a DJ on his way to his own chat show or the Eurovision Song Contest or Saturday morning kids' TV. Or even a BAFTA for best DJ of the moment. He was in it for the rock'n'roll. What else was there? His dad believed in higher things – but you had to just take what you could get now. That's all Jake could see.

The kitchen went quiet. He noticed that immediately.

'You switched off the radio didn't you?'

'Of course.' She'd flicked a switch while he'd been busy thinking.

'What d'you mean – of course? I was listening to that.'

'No, you weren't. You've been outside. Mooching in the morgue.'

'It's not a morgue, it's a graveyard. And I could hear it outside, and anyway I was intending to be inside soon. To listen to it.'

He switched it back on. Mink DeVille were singing 'Spanish stroll'.

'Turn it off, we need to talk.'

'We can talk with it on.'

'No, we can't. You'll start telling me stupid statistics about how many hits the Buzzcocks had.'

'It's not the Buzzcocks, it's Mink DeVille.'

'See? You're at it already.'

'But I thought you loved music.'

'Yeah. Just not like you. Turn it off.'

'I can't – not in the middle.'

'What?'

'I can't switch it off in the middle of a track. Have the decency to wait for them to stop playing.'

'They're not playing! It's some stupid DJ in some tin-box studio with a computer that picks the tracks for him.'

Jake chewed his lip and frowned. 'It's stupid DJs like that who can save lives.'

'Turn it off.'

'I'll fade it out.'

'What?'

'I'll have the decency to give Mink DeVille a respectful fade-out then at least it'll seem as if the track was ending prematurely.'

'I wish you'd end prematurely sometimes. I'm pregnant.'

Jake stared.

'It might be twins. There are twins in my family and yours.'

Jake stared.

'Well, say something . . . *Dad.*'

'Are you sure?' Jake looked incredibly pale.

She nodded. 'I did a test. You don't look . . . over the moon.'

'It's a shock. I thought you were on the pill.'

'I thought I was on the pill.'

His face was like white granite, he was slipping into a daze. 'I don't wanna be tied down.'

'Too late.'

Jake's life flashed before his eyes. The life he'd never have. The freedom to laze about in his own graveyard, listening to the birds and watching the mist caress the stones. The idle afternoons lounging in pubs and coffee houses picking up the latest stories and gossip for his daily show. The long nights organising playlists and letting the new music pound his ear drums. Little children wouldn't let him do all that. They'd keep him up all right, but not so he could lounge about in Popland. Suddenly it felt like his life was over: the walls weren't just closing in, they were crashing down on him. He felt the need to run.

'Say something, Jake.'

'I was gonna have you on my show, get you to meet famous Dave.'

'You still can. I still wanna meet Dave.'

'But what's the point? You'll be home wiping up sick and sterilising bottles. You won't have time for a serious music career. Why did you do this? Surely it wasn't on purpose?'

She walked over and calmly slapped his face, leaving a fierce imprint on his left cheek and an insistent buzz in his ear.

'Stop being an idiot,' she said. 'You can't run forever, Jake. You can't avoid responsibility. Plenty of people have kids and go on to lead perfectly normal lives.'

'But I don't want a normal life. I want an extraordinary life. I want to change the world, and lift people out of their mire through the magic of music. I don't want to be the one in the mire. Who's gonna lift me out?'

She shook her head, slapped him one more time, then turned and left the kitchen. Jake poured a large whisky and went and sat amongst the dead. This was serious. And that was when he decided he had to get out. He really was going to run.

'That was Camera Shy and "Don't point that thing at me", this is Testing for Sharks with "Legless".'

Jake was going through the motions tonight. He couldn't get the baby out of his head. His main problem was that he usually talked on air about whatever was rattling around in his biscuit-tin brain: radio was therapy for him. But not with this. How could he talk about this? It was too raw, too frightening. To talk about it might make it happen, although he clearly did understand how you really made these kinds of things happen. But speaking out loud about it might just make it worse. He wanted to talk to Rach about it too. He was pinning his hopes on meeting her outside the Ladder, as the sun went down.

'That was Mad Kevin and "His white sox" and this is the BobyZos.' No facts, no anecdotes, no circular rock-'n'roll stories. Just music. Plain old decent song after decent song. There was something honest, something pure, something therapeutic even about just rattling out the good solid tunes without the banter.

'Here's the new one from the Smashing Pipkins.'

It was his shield against the world. His shield against reality and fatherhood.

He only just made it through the show that night.

'Stick around average punters, 'cause we've got the Waterbottles on the way, straight after Lawrence of Olivier with "Sand and Shakespeare".'

'Some guy called Easy called.'

Jake nearly leapt out of skin. It was late and he'd just got in. He'd expected the chapel to be as quiet as its many graves but Leah was sitting at the large pine kitchen table, flipping through maternity magazines. Magazines solved everything for Leah: if they did a glossy mag on Jake she'd have bought a lifetime subscription. Jake glanced at the clock, it was midnight.

'Easy?'

'Yep, didn't sound *easy* though. Sounded mad. Sounded ready to kill something.'

'What did he say?'

'He said to tell you Easy called and he'd be calling again.'

Easy was his dad's nickname for his brother. That clinched it then. He'd have to find a way to get out; his life was closing in on him. First the baby, now this.

And there was no doubt Easy was ready to kill something. Or someone.

Jake sneaked off to bed, leaving Leah looking at foetal scans.

Disintegrating

Sol felt as if he was disintegrating, collapsing from the inside out. Oh, you'd never have known: he was too good an actor, in the worst sense. Whenever he was with other people his survival instinct kicked in and the shutters closed. Hi-tech, good-looking, all-knowing, confident shutters. But truth be told, his soul was folding in on itself like a tower of cards.

He rolled over and stared at another picture-perfect face, another one-night bland. Not the girl's fault: he'd not let her over the reality threshold. There was nothing of interest in what they'd done because it was just two-dimensional bump and grind, sex without the shadows, no honesty, no history, no soul. Two bodies making the most of gravity. That was all. A few ups and downs before saying see ya later, with no real intention of the *later* bit at all. It was supposed to be some kind of anaesthetic, but as Sol lay there in the dark he knew it was just exacerbating the pain. If life was only this then he didn't want it, having everything had somehow resulted in him having nothing. He was just a shell: no hopes, no dreams, no direction, no purpose. Nothing meant anything.

He got up, sat with his head in his hands for a while, then went to the kitchen and poured himself a sizeable whisky.

He'd downed half of it when she appeared in the doorway.

'Got any for me?'

Clang. Those shutters slammed faster than a steel trap. He grinned and winked at her. 'Sure.'

'I have a boyfriend.'

'Oh. Lucky you.'

'You mean it doesn't bother you?'

'Not unless he goes by the name of Goliath.'

He handed her a smaller version of the drink in his hand.

'In some countries they consider it an insult to offer the guest the smaller portion,' she said, sniffing and rubbing a hand through her hair.

She had a fascinating face, and a way of tilting her head and squinting at him as if he was standing in the sun. He couldn't decide if he loved or hated it.

He sighed and offered her his own glass. She took it. Without thinking he topped up the one he'd offered her.

'Nice flat you got.'

'I can afford it,' he said.

'Obviously. Let's see – stockbroker?'

He laughed. 'No – silver spoon. My dad's a world-class musician. If he never worked again I'd still not need to lift a finger to earn a dime.'

'Cool.'

'No. Not cool. Not cool at all.' And suddenly it felt as if the shutters were buckling and the brick mask was starting to crumble. He turned and stared at her. 'D'you ever feel like it's all useless?'

'No.'

'Well, does your boyfriend then?'

'What?'

She did that head-tilt squinting thing again, and he realised right then – he hated it.

'I haven't got anything left to do. I've done it all. I'm twenty-seven... and I've been there, done it, bought the

T-shirt and thrown up all over it. D'you know how frightening that is?'

She scowled. 'I only wanted a whisky,' she said.

'So did I,' he muttered, and he swallowed another mouthful.

'Look, I'm sorry,' he said. 'I didn't mean to freak you out.'

Another hateful head tilt.

'You didn't freak me. To be honest I wasn't sure there was any flesh and blood in there. Makes a change to find a bloke who'll be a bit more honest.'

He snorted into his Jack Daniels 'Honest! Honest! You have no idea.'

'What d'you mean?'

The whisky was going to his head, joyriding around his brain and making his thoughts spin.

'I mean . . . I mean . . . I can't even say what I mean. I'm locked inside myself and I used to like it like that and now I hate it.' He walked round the kitchen, running the tips of his fingers across the surfaces. 'It's like, it's like, I'm the movie and you're the audience. Like I . . . I wanted to be in my own little show and now I'm trapped in it. And the reviews have been terrible but I can't stop it. No one's interested in it but I can't stop performing it. Night after night after night.'

She gave a sly smile. 'The performance looked pretty good to me,' she said.

He frowned. 'You don't get it, do you?'

She shrugged and thought for a moment. 'Try growing up,' she said suddenly.

So he picked up the Jack Daniels bottle and flung it at her. Something in him, some survival instinct, forced him to miss, but it shocked the both of them. She turned in slow motion and stared at the glistening stain on the wall.

'You bastard.'

'Look, I'm sorry, I . . .'

He didn't get another word out. He couldn't: she had slammed her hand across his mouth.

The key

Cain lay in bed, sleepless. The clock said 12.45 am. but he knew it was lying. It was at least two in the morning. He rolled his head and glanced up at the ceiling. There was a tiny key hooked on one of the beams up there, just below the massive cobweb.

Who would hang a key up high like that, and why? He'd have to check it sometime. No, he'd check it now. He had nothing else to do. He stood up and unhooked it. His height made it easy to get hold of. He was examining it when there was a noise downstairs. A creak or footstep or one of the walls groaning a little. He hated moments like these. Especially in such a spooky house. He listened again. Another creak. He put the key back and leapt off the bed. He reached underneath the bed and slid out a metal baseball bat. You couldn't be too careful. People could come looking for you; you never knew when the past might leap out and crush your skull with its bare hands. All those little mistakes and regrets, lying in wait, ready to gang up on him and bury him alive one day.

He pulled on a jumper and his jeans and took up the bat. Then he crept to the door and peered into the corridor that ran the length of the landing. For a moment he felt like a little boy again. Peeking out on his parents as they had another argument about the past, and who was to blame. He'd sat at the top of those stairs so many

The key

times it had almost become a cosy ritual. Not to hear his parents howling at each other – that just gave him a sick feeling in his stomach – but once he realised they wouldn't kill each other, once he knew this was part of who they were, then it became a kind of regular feature, something that made him feel life was OK, he was OK. He'd sit in his own little cocoon, wrapped in the duvet, staring at the wall through the stair rails and listening.

And that's what he did now. Without the duvet. With a baseball bat instead. He sat at the top of the stairs and listened. Another creak from down below. He'd have to investigate or he'd never get any sleep. His imagination was a powerful beast, a tormenting intruder that would not let him rest. It kept jabbing a white-hot poker into his brain, feeding him the kind of images Spielberg would die for. It was ridiculous, he was six foot, and bigger than most things in this poky little cottage. He steeled himself and inched down the old carpeted stairs. They came out into the dining room, and the place was full of moonlight and shade and the kind of shadows that suggested the darkness contained deformed creatures with teeth the size of nuclear missiles. He reached for the light switch and flicked it down. A sudden flash of yellow and then blackness. The bulb was dead. He shivered. He had no idea whether there were any spares; he'd certainly not bought any.

He now had to cross the length of the room in the dark, to reach the kitchen light. He gripped the bat, hugging it to his chest. His shoulder brushed the curtain and a flash of moonlight lit up the whole room momentarily. Of course. The moon: that was as good as a torch right now. He grabbed the curtain and flung it back. The room was bathed in white light. And Cain saw what had made the noise. There was a woman standing there. A girl bathed in moonlight, dressed in white and smiling at him. Holding a hand out to him. He swallowed and backed up against the wall. The bat nudged a vase and there was a crash as something expensive lost its value. He stepped sideways and his naked foot connected with the shards of pottery. He could feel the jagged spikes digging into the soft flesh between his toes. He glanced down then looked up, and in that instant the girl vanished, silently, effortlessly. Was she in the kitchen? He crossed the room like a shot and hit the light. The place was empty. And the bathroom beyond too. Cain massaged his eyes and leant against the sink.

Was he going mad? He pulled his hands away from his eyes: they were covered in thick congealed blood. He ran to the mirror and checked his face. Nothing. When he looked back at his hands they were clean. Something flashed in the mirror and he spun round. Was it the girl again? There was no one. He checked the front door in the dining room – the only entrance to the cottage – but it was locked. No one had broken in. He gave a cursory glance towards the cracked back window, but it was still intact. He went back to bed. Yet he didn't sleep a wink.

Jake's women

Jake would never have admitted it out loud but there were times when he needed, so needed, these women. As inconvenient and precarious as it often was. When he was on the radio he was in his element – his own world of wires and sliders and music and trivia and interviews – but at the other times, in other people's worlds, he was lost and desperately needed a translator, someone to help him do the simple things. Match clothes, fill in forms, ask for directions, make small talk. These complex tasks were sometimes way beyond him and left him feeling lost and bewildered. That's when he needed Rach and Leah to make sense of his world. He loved the idea of freedom, but at times when he found himself alone and free, he couldn't stop longing for some boundaries.

He just had to make sure, that whatever happened, his women never found out about each other. If they did, he might lose them both.

'No one knows where she is, stupid cow. She could be anywhere.'
  'What?' Jake rolled over in bed and looked at Leah. It was half past midnight and she was staring at a photo of Rach. 'Oh! Your sister!' he swallowed hard. 'Yeah, right.'
  'Well, sound like you care. I mean, I know you never met her but . . .'

'No.'

'What d'you mean "no"?' she said. 'No what? What d'you mean?'

'What d'you mean – what do I mean? I just mean "no".'

'No what?'

'No, I never met her.'

Leah rolled her eyes. 'I know that,' she said, 'but you could look as if you're interested.' She turned and set her piercing gaze in his direction.

Jake flinched. 'I don't know her,' he said.

'I'm not asking you to know her.'

'Leah! There's a million homeless people out there.'

'So?'

'So I'm just saying.'

'Saying what? She's not homeless.'

'What?'

'She's in Asia somewhere.'

'Asia!' he yelled.

'Yeah, Asia. Don't strain your groin. One day she'll be back. Stupid cow.'

Leah rolled her eyes and turned over. Jake couldn't help but smile to himself. Asia?

'You're in Asia. That must be nice.'

Rach stared at him. It was the following evening, around ten, and they were sat outside The Ladder in a fine drizzle. Rach's left cheek was streaked with something yellow and the rain was moistening it and making it seep down her face. She opened her mouth to reply but just went on staring. It started to unnerve him.

Eventually she said, 'You've been talking to my sister.'

'I just heard, that's all.'

'How d'you know Leah?'

'I don't.'

'Oh my . . . you're sleeping with her.'
'I am not.'
'You are.'

Jake stood up: he was cornered now. Women had too much intuition, made too many assumptions, put two and two together before he'd even got his calculator out. He sighed. 'I'm off home,' he said.

The year was moving on: the summer had been as bad as ever and Father Time had been out with his perennial blowtorch, setting the moor alight with the first flames of autumn. The wind was whipping up the night, stealing the day away far too early.

'Come if you want,' he said, 'but I'm not sitting out here any more. I'm cold.'

'You know I don't do that.'

'Do what?'

'Go home with strange men.'

'I'm not a strange man.' He was walking away now.

'I'm not sure now. Two minutes ago you'd never heard of Leah.'

'That's not true – you never stop going on about her.'

She leapt up and ran after him, tugging at his sleeve like a five year old. 'That's a lie. I don't like talking about her. Stupid cow.'

'Why d'you hate each other?'

'We don't.'

'But it's always *stupid cow*, the only time you two ever . . .' He stopped and carried on walking. He was saying too much.

'Like I say,' he said, 'I'm going home. Come if you want. You'll be impressed. I have a whole churchyard to myself. You can sleep behind one of the gravestones if you like.'

'I don't wanna meet *her*.'

'She's not there.'

He turned and stared at Rach. He was bluffing of course, and she could see it.

'I don't believe you,' she said. 'You lied about knowing her.'

'I don't know her.'

In one sense that was true. Leah was always elusive. He'd been in her body many times – but never really in her head.

He'd explored her physique to the nth degree, he'd get a BA in her anatomy if one were available – but he'd never once been inside her head. Leah's mind was a foreign country and he couldn't get a visa. She and Jake seemed to inhabit two entirely different continents.

Rach, on the other hand, was another trip entirely: her mind was an internet café with twenty-four-hour access, it was her body that was beyond reach. That seemed to be a dangerous place strewn with landmines and broken glass. He'd never get in there and come out alive. He'd never get in there full stop.

Revelations

Leah was standing framed in the chapel doorway as he trudged up the path. It was just as well Rach had refused to come back with him: Leah would have been the first thing she'd seen.

'How d'you manage to live here? Old wrecks like this cost a fortune,' she asked him as he slipped past her. 'I mean it's not as if Sunshine Radio has made you an A-list celebrity. And surely it's owned by the National Front anyway.'

'What is?'

'All this land.'

'You're kidding me . . .'

'No, the National Front own loads of stuff.'

'The National Trust! You airhead.'

Leah shrugged. 'Same difference,' she said.

Jake smiled. 'I have means,' he said.

'What means?'

'Just means. And I may not be A-list but I have been invited to Noddy Holder's birthday bash. And I can take a guest. So treat me right.'

'How d'you manage to live in that chapel?' Rach asked him the next night. 'I bet a place like that must cost a packet.'

He thought for a moment. 'D'you wanna know the truth? It isn't pretty.'

'I can trade you a hundred ugly stories for your one.'

'I stole it,' he said.

Her eyes widened. 'You stole a chapel?'

'Well, no, I stole the money to buy it. Straight up. I ran off with the inheritance that was supposed to go to my brother. Ran away and spent it all on that spooky wreck.'

'It's not a spooky wreck.'

'How would you know? You've never been there. You never come with me.'

'I spy on you. Your brother's gonna kill you.'

Jake nodded, his face dark. 'That's why he can never find me. Believe me, if he ever gets wind of where I am, I'm a dead man. Problem is – I think he's coming. I may have to get out. D'you really spy on me?'

'Sometimes. I've never seen *her* though. Does she live there?'

He sat back and nodded, discomfort sweeping across his features.

'A lot of the time,' he said.

Rach nodded. 'I thought so. Just don't tell her about me,' she said and she got up and started to limp away. Then she stopped and turned. 'Ever,' she said with emphasis. 'Or I'll have to get out and you'll never see me again. She's as jealous as hell and would ruin both of us.' She paused and thought for a moment, then said, 'D'you hate your brother?'

'D'you hate your sister?' Jake replied.

She shook her head. 'Not really.'

'Me neither. We just fell out a few years back and never patched it up and the longer it went on the harder it got. Eventually I couldn't stand being around at home, my dad tends to side with my brother, so I saw a way to get out. Esau had a lot of money coming to him – a long promised endowment from the old man. Esau's not the sharpest signal on the dial. It wasn't difficult to steal it. I went out while everyone slept peacefully one night and just ran off and bought the spooky wreck.'

He watched her limp away, a little hunched figure, old beyond her years. Then, when it was just him and the night and the ponies he sat in silence for a while and wondered what it was like to be a dad. The word was short but it felt very heavy to him, so loaded. He wondered if he'd feel the same if the baby was Rach's. Maybe. Maybe not.

This revelation from Leah had upset the equilibrium now. A baby changed everything.

He knew what he'd do: he'd get this audition with Leah and Sol done and dusted, get the girl the break, then he'd pack a bag, nothing bulky, and slip out into the night, buy himself some thinking time. Leah would have a career in the making, something to fall back on, and he could think about setting up somewhere else. It wasn't the first time he'd dreamt up this plan and it wouldn't be the last. But it made him feel a hell of a lot better to have it in his head like a little escape hatch.

Sol was as good as his word: he searched, he asked around, he phoned and he googled – but he found nothing. Abby had disappeared. Her face had been lifted from the planet. He asked in the local pubs and the city clubs, he had a small creased photo printed from Dave's phone, and he gave it a lot of air time, but no one knew anything. It was as if Abby just didn't exist any more.

OCD

'Once again I find myself with no sense of order at all in my life. I've ended up yet again with no world of my own, no safe place, every bit of the planet belongs to someone else, feels like I'm always trespassing. Always in fear of contamination and unacceptability. Of course that's probably all to do with the obsessive compulsive disorder. I can pinpoint the very day the virus took hold, the day the poison started leaking into my brain. Twelve, I was – very young to start on the self-destruction highway. The road to nowhere. Dad had complained about greasy fingerprints on the car door handle. My old man worshipped that car, and I – I worshipped my old man. So I dutifully complied and scrubbed the car clean. Not just the handle, the whole shooting match, and then my hands, ten, maybe fifteen times, before the sun went down. I've been doing it ever since, trying to keep my hands clean, trying not to contaminate things I touch. Sometimes I get away with it, sometimes people notice.'

Cain stared at his reflection in the mirror beside the door. There was no one there to hear his monologue, of course. Talking to himself was a regular occurrence these days.

'What's that stain?' Tamar asked him while he was washing glasses one day.

She was like that: eyes like a hawk. He got away with nothing when she was around.

Cain studied the back of his hand. He'd noticed it getting more pronounced. 'I dunno,' he muttered, giving it a quick rub, 'can't seem to get rid of it.'

'Maybe you should see the doctor, might be serious.'

He shrugged and acted as if it meant nothing to him. But later that night he washed his hand repeatedly. Sixteen times in half an hour.

He couldn't get rid of the smear. He didn't know where it had come from or what it meant. It wasn't oil, wasn't a burn, or a bruise. It wasn't a scar. He scrubbed and scrubbed and scrubbed but it wouldn't go, it just wouldn't go. In the end the back of his hand was so raw, he had to stop trying.

That night, when he locked the door of the cottage, he checked the lock six times. Then he went back and checked it a further four. He had to, in his mind the fear of punishment from the all-seeing creator always loomed larger at times like this. In moments of great stress, the OCD was most intense. It clawed at his head like a ravenous wolf, threatening to devour his sanity and bring the full weight of the heavens down on him.

He checked the bathroom taps for any drips, and those in the kitchen as well, waving his hand underneath and reciting his appropriate words, words he'd been saying for years, words that would somehow make it all right. Eventually he felt released enough to go to bed. But the process took a while, much longer than usual.

Laban

Leah was sitting by Mo Mountain's grave, strumming through some happy chords. As soon as she saw Jake appear on the gravel path, snaking between the tombstone labyrinth, she called out to him. 'Dad's coming.'

'Good evening to you, too,' he said. 'Whose dad?'

'Mine. He wants to meet you. He's coming over from the city.'

Jake stopped. Meeting in-laws was serious. Meeting in-laws meant long-term prospects and future Christmases spent at each other's houses. 'Why's he want to meet me?'

'Cause I love you,' Leah said, and she gave him a broad wink.

Jake's face fell through the floor. 'I'm not ready,' he said.

'Course you are, you have to be, he'll be here in half an hour.'

'You're kidding, we've got nothing to eat.'

'Oh yes, we do. I went out and I bought stuff and it's cooking right now. I even bought cigars and brandy.'

'I don't like cigars and brandy.'

'They're not for you.'

Laban Paddan, not the sort of name you said quickly after a few glasses of wine, was a big man. In all senses. He oozed confidence, power and his own special personality.

He wore a pinstriped suit, fat braces, a loud cravat, and gold bracelets. He was a self-made man, and he knew it.

'Grieves me no end to see you in this squalor,' he said as Leah served up lamb casserole with five different vegetables.

'I rather like this place,' Jake muttered. He'd resolved to be restrained and courteous, keep his head down and run for cover as soon as possible.

Laban sighed noisily and shook his head. 'I suppose it's ... original,' he said and he filled his mouth with lamb.

Leah poured him a third glass of red wine.

'So Leah tells me you're a DJ in your spare time?'

'No, all the time.'

'All the time?'

'Yeah, it's my job.'

'But can you make a living doing that? I mean I know the guys at the BBC do but you're not at the BBC, are you?'

'Not yet,' said Jake. 'But I do all right. And I have means.'

Laban raised his thick eyebrows. 'Means?'

'My family ... I,' a quick glance at Leah, 'inherited.'

Laban grimaced, stuffed his mouth and chewed noisily. 'Good lamb,' he said, through the mouthful of green and brown.

Silence. Apart from the chewing and drinking. Then,

'So, Jake, what do you do the rest of the time?' Laban asked, prising strands of meat from between his front teeth.

'Not a lot. Being a DJ takes up a lot of it.'

'But Leah says you're only on the air two hours a day.'

'Yes, but I have to plan the shows, set up interviews, choose music, gather trivia.'

'Gather trivia?' Laban shook his head and then drained his glass. He opened his mouth to comment, then shut it again. The meeting was not travelling on an upward trajectory.

'It takes time to put together a quality show,' Jake said.

'Why do they play all that rubbish then? When they've got all day to choose the music?'

Jake bit his lip, cleared his throat aggressively and said, 'So, what music do you like, Mr Paddan?'

'I don't. I've no time for swanning about with a radio, I've got a thriving business to maintain. I didn't build it up from scratch listening to Pick of the Pops.'

Jake wilted visibly. It was a losing battle. He said nothing.

'No news on your sister then?' Laban said to his daughter.

'Are you asking or telling, Dad?'

'I'm just saying. No news. I've put out adverts, paid investigators and hired bounty hunters. If she's in Asia, she's found a good hiding place.'

'Asia's massive,' Jake said, 'and mysterious.'

'And no place for Rachel. Poor kid. She'd better be home soon or I'll have something to say when she does get back'

'She's a free agent, Dad.'

'Yeah, but so are you and you haven't gone native, have you?'

'Maybe she's closer to home,' Jake said.

Laban stopped chewing and stared at him. 'What's that supposed to mean?'

Jake swallowed hard and shrugged. 'Maybe she's . . . in Europe. Or Scotland.'

'Don't be stupid. Why would she go to Scotland? Why would she leave home at all? Silly cow.'

Jake chewed slowly and stared at the big man in the pinstripes. He could answer that question quite easily but he chose not to.

Afterwards Leah volunteered to wash up, not a good sign, whilst Jake and Laban crashed out in two massive armchairs in the snug (it used to be the transept to the left of the huge stone pulpit). The transept to the right was now Jake's office and his portal to every single bit of music on the world wide web. The chancel at the front, where many poor choir boys had dozed over the years, had appropriately been walled off to make Jake's bedroom, and the nave (where the pulpit still towered way above contradiction and where everyone else had regularly dozed) had become a spacious kitchen, lounge and dining room in one. Jake had shown Leah's old man around with a certain amount of pride. Laban had frowned a lot and said little, though he did enjoy an indulgent moment of glory up in the pulpit. Back in the snug, Jake poured brandies and Laban lit up a cigar the size of a chair leg.

'So, Jake,' Laban flexed his ample frame in the armchair, and big as the seat was it struggled to hold him. 'Let's talk man to man.'

Jake scowled and sank down in his seat. He took a gulp of the brandy. It was good stuff.

'When you gonna make an honest woman of her?' Laban asked.

Jake blinked and said, 'Who?'

'Oh, don't play the innocent, Jake. Leah. She's knocked up, I know it, you know it, she knows it. When you gonna do the decent thing? When you gonna pop the question?'

Jake's jaw flapped open. 'Er . . . soon . . . probably.'

'There ain't no "probably" or "soon" about it, son. I learnt early on in life – you gotta decide what you want and go for it. Don't pussyfoot about on the edge. And with my Leah it's all there for you. A good job in the company – quite high up – shift the two of you out of this dump – proper showbiz wedding.'

'I don't want a showbiz wedding – and what's wrong with this dump?'

'Well, look at it. You can't bring a kid up here. The place is as damp as a tramp's trousers.'

'It is not. I'd love to have grown up in a place like this. It's got magic, it's got atmosphere.'

'Jake! Jake! Jake!' Laban leant forward in his chair and waved his cigar about. 'Kids don't want atmosphere. They want warmth and health and all mod cons.'

'Not love, then?'

'Jake, you're a romantic, son, life doesn't work like that. Love only gets you so far, I hear what you're saying, believe me I do.' Laban sobered up for a moment and stared Jake full in the face. 'Look at me, son. Take my advice, it's commitment that matters. Knuckle down, get a job with me and marry the girl. Believe me, you can't do better than Leah.'

And the moment Laban said it, Rach flashed into Jake's mind. He couldn't help it or control it. It just happened. Jake stared back at his prospective father-in-law, but all he could see was Rach.

PART THREE

Haggy

Haggy Smack was a legend. He and Dave had made musical history together. Haggy had been cutting records since the dawn of record cutting, and he'd worked with the best. He sat there now in Dave's studio, purple shades perched on his sun-strafed nose while a dead spliff hung from his charred lips.

'Once spent five weeks in the Orient with Jagger,' he rasped, the joint bouncing up and down as he talked, 'recording an album that never saw the light of day. Shining Shenanigans it was gonna be called, lost treasure, misplaced bounty. Watch this space, kid, it'll happen. Only took three sessions then we spent the rest of the time impressing women and working on maintaining a perpetual high. One day some young musical Indiana Jones will rediscover it and make a mint.'

He genuinely didn't seem bothered whether it saw daylight or not, he just seemed to like the story.

They sat in hallowed silence listening to the recording of Haggy's latest track, a recording they'd just cut. A full 4 minutes 51 seconds of jangling guitars and soaring chords, then 30 seconds of silence before the approving grunts and nods and gentle cries of, 'Cool, man. Cool.'

Ten minutes later, when the mumbled accolades had dried up, Sol found himself alone with the gnarled Haggy while his dad went out for a ponder. The recording was good, it just lacked . . . something.

'Your old man and me – we go back a long way. All the way to the dawn of time,' Haggy growled.

Sol knew this speech, he'd heard it a hundred times and could fill in any gaps should Haggy's potholed memory fail him.

'The dawn of time as far as music goes, anyways. You know, your old man worked his way up from nothing. Nothing. His old man was just a factory worker. Nothing wrong with that, of course – but everything you see now, this rock'n'roll empire – it all came from sweat and tears and grinding. You've had it so easy, kid. So easy. Everything's come to you on a silver turntable. You were born with a gold disc in your mouth. King Dave wasn't. He had to work his way up from ground zero. Never forget that. Never take it for granted.'

Haggy sat back in his seat and belched. Then he pulled out a massive slice of cigarette paper and rolled himself something huge and fragrant. Sol said nothing; he knew better than that. The speech wasn't done yet.

'And one day, boy, this'll all be yours, this dynasty will fall on your shoulders. Not on your brother's, on yours. You're the one. Not some accountant up north. He may come sniffing after the money – but you're the one with the vision. You'll be the next king of rock'n'roll round here. Strengthen those shoulders. 'Cause it's a weight. The Beatles, the Stones, Spector, the Beach Boys, the Pistols, Floyd . . . you have a lot to live up to.' Then he did the usual gesture and Sol was invited to speak. So he said what he always said at this juncture.

'I'm not a musician, Haggy. I'm a people man. I can spot the songs and the singers. But I can't make the music.'

Haggy nodded drunkenly. 'Exactly, which is why you need me. Your dad's right-hand man.'

And he leant forward and leered at Sol. Sol considered, then said what he'd always wanted to say at this point.

'Haggy, you'll be long gone before my old man's corpse ever hits the bottom of a grave.'

Haggy's face froze. He didn't like that. Not one bit. 'You know nothing, kid,' was all he said, but Sol had a hunch that if he'd been packing a gun there'd have been six holes down his chest right then. A line of bloody button holes peppering his T-shirt.

'I know one thing,' Sol said, 'I'm gonna build a proper studio, a whacking great place in its own grounds – the kind of place everyone will want to come and record in. It'll be the standard – everything else that's gone before will be in its shadow.'

'Don't be a freak,' Haggy growled back, and then fell into a coughing fit, 'Why d'you need some monument like that? It's the music that matters. People'll think you got something to hide.'

'I got something to celebrate – something worth a proper palace. No more squeezing into this shoebox, worrying about the neighbours. I'll really put Radio Therapy on the map. Everyone'll know the name.'

'Ha! Everyone already knows the name. The music already put it on the map.'

'OK boys, everyone happy?' Dave said, bustling back in, rubbing his hands, the sure signal he'd found the missing ingredient.

Haggy and Sol looked up at Dave and hid their scowls.

'Sure, Dad, let's finish this sucker.'

'Er, s'cuse me.' Before they could continue a uniformed officer appeared in the doorway. Policemen looked younger by the day. This one was clearly thirteen.

'Can we help you, officer?' Sol's dad was nothing if not polite.

Haggy was nothing if not guilty. His face turned three shades of green and he swallowed the spliff in one.

'D'you know an Abby Mann?' the officer said.

Sol cleared his throat and blanched a little. 'Yeah . . . sure. Not well . . . but . . .'

'We're trying to track her down at the moment. We found this address in her book.'

Dave looked at Sol and raised an eyebrow, looking for all the world like Roger Moore.

After the thirteen-year-old had gone, and Haggy was wandering around on the pavement outside trying to remember where he left his Harley, Dave sat his son down in the studio and pushed a whisky into his hand.

'No joy on Abby, then?'

Sol shook his head. 'Not really. Though I found a guy in Peniel Green who may know something. Her big brother.'

Dave shook his head. 'Doesn't look good,' he said. 'Sweet kid, too. Wouldn't hurt a fly. Why would she take off like this?'

Sol shrugged. 'If the police are involved then something's really rotten in Denmark. We have to find her.'

Sol looked pained and Dave raised another eyebrow. 'You haven't . . . you didn't sleep with her?' Dave said. 'This isn't a scam on your part, is it?'

'I've slept with a lot of people lately.'

Dave did his Roger Moore again. 'I hope you've been careful?' he said.

Sol let out a cynical snort. 'Depends. If you mean have I left a trail of impregnated women – no. If you mean have I screwed up them and me. Yeah, probably. Everything's falling apart.'

'How come?'

'I dunno. Some days I can't see the point. People work and play, fight and make up, the sun rises and dies again, rivers flood and dry up . . .'

'That's the line!'

'What?'

'That song you wrote. The one you gave me – we were short a line. Quick.' He scooped up a pen and a nearby CD sleeve and tried to scribble. The pen was dry so he grabbed a marker and daubed across his arm. '"Rivers flood and dry, the sun rises and dies in the sky." Perfect. Scans too I reckon.' He hummed to himself for a second.

'How can you still be so enthusiastic, Dad? After all these years, all those songs, all those hits and misses? How can you still get excited about a couple of lines? It changes nothing. And what about Abby?'

Dave grinned at him.

'That's where you're wrong. The beauty of this thing is we don't know.'

'We don't know?'

'We don't know what and who it changes. Some waster may hear your song one day and pick himself up out of the gutter and start his life again. Some heartbroken wife, dumped by too many men, might find the strength to carry on. You never know.'

'That's not beautiful, that's a bummer.'

'No, Sol, it's poetry, it's what we do. The little things. I'd have given up years ago if I didn't think the little things changed the world. For every poster hero who's supposed to make something happen, there's a million unknown losers who did the little things that really made life worth living. Believe it, Sol.'

'*You're* a poster hero, Dad.'

'Exactly. So what does that tell you?'

Sol grimaced and stood up. 'I don't know. I'm fed up of all these theories, all this poetry. Seems like all these songs, all this philosophy and poetry are just so many conspiracy theories about what makes the world turn. Doesn't make you feel better about it all.'

'Don't turn your back on your maker, Sol. You need him.'

'Do I? I wouldn't know, I've got so much other stuff in the way . . . I'm gonna take off for a few days. Run away for a bit. Get my head together. If I find Abby in the process, I'll let you know.'

Two days later Sol got a call.

'Sol – where are you? Still around? Come over, I got someone who wants to meet you. This'll lift you out of your slough of despair.'

Sol was packing at the time. Not much: just a few things in a designer rucksack.

'Who is it?'

'You won't be disappointed, son. Come over.'

'But I've got a cab waiting . . .'

Too late. His old man had hung up. Sol sighed, finished his packing and threw the bag in the back of the waiting taxi. He'd drop in on his old man on the way to the station.

Wherever you go

Dave was practically glowing when Sol walked in the door. Radio Therapy Records was pungent with the aroma of alcohol, Calvin Klein perfume and Cuban cigars. Dave's dad didn't smoke Cuban so whoever had come visiting clearly did. She was upstairs in the studio, draped in a chair in red leather trousers and a huge fur coat. Her face was like an oil painting, all red gashes and black lines. Underneath it Sol was sure there was a beautiful woman, but she was clearly taking no chances.

'Sol, my boy,' (it was always 'my boy' when his dad was in the presence of pop greatness) 'this is Sheba.'

Sol stared. 'Yeah, I know.'

Sheba didn't get up, but she did crack a warm smile. Sol spotted the two black minders lurking in the background.

'How's it going?' Sol asked, not quite sure of the appropriate greeting.

'Cool, it's going cool. You're doing well too. I hear a lot about you these days.'

Sheba had an irresistible voice: it was like smoky cream. Sol knew that because he'd written it in a review somewhere.

'In the words of Fatboy Slim – you've come a long way, baby,' Sol quipped and Sheba laughed. Underneath all that gloss she was still the same sassy individual.

'Fame hasn't changed you much then,' he added, nodding towards the minders and gesturing at her clothes.

'Meteoric success comes with a price, my boy,' his dad said.

Sol scowled. 'How many albums is it then? Twenty million worldwide?'

'Twenty-five and counting,' Dave said.

Sol was hoping Sheba might still have the grace to blush, but it was hard to tell under all that slap. 'I hope you tell everyone it was all down to me,' Sol said and she laughed her smoky laugh again. 'I mean if I hadn't nipped into that pub that night to get away from my nagging mum . . . karaoke's a wonderful thing, eh?'

'Sol,' Sheba stood up, rising like the Statue of Liberty on the horizon. Man, she was tall. Like an urban goddess, and with the heels on those boots she was more Amazonian than ever. She glided across the floor towards Sol, and slipped an arm around his shoulder, her hand slithering across his neck like a snake. Somewhere in her past there was Egyptian blood and she still carried herself like a Pharaoh's daughter.

'Sol – I want some new songs. You know how it is. Triumphant first album, everybody loves you, eats out of your hand, critics come gagging to slobber all over your snakeskin boots.'

He knew what was coming.

'But one day you wake up and realise you're staring it in the face – that difficult second album. The maturing. That's what I need Sol, fourteen great tunes that will keep everyone happy.'

Sol shook his head. 'Can't be done,' he said.

Dave drew in a sharp breath and held up a hand. 'Easy kid – for people like Sheba anything can be done.'

Sheba stooped a little and stared him straight in the eye. 'And Sol – if anyone can do it – it's you.'

But Sol shook his head. She was so close to him now it was starting to make him feel drunk. But he wouldn't lose his head over this woman. He stared back at her, into those clear crystal eyes and he was relieved to see she really was still there under the wall of glamour.

'You have to decide Sheba – the maturing or the fourteen great tunes – the kids or the critics. You can't please everyone. Not even Shakey could do that.'

She pulled away. 'Shakey who?'

'Shakespeare. Sheba, if you want another megabucks album, hang out with some Boys 'R' Us Band or some other shiny new popsters. You'll find plenty of toe-tapping tunes out there. But if you want something metal to stick on your mantelpiece and glowing reviews in *The Guardian* then I can suggest a few people.'

She jabbed a long finger into his chest. Sheba's nails went on forever and he felt the sharp edge through his shirt. 'I don't want a few people Sol, I want you. The boy wonder. That's why I came to this little dump.'

Dave winced and, somewhere in the background, one of the minders shrugged apologetically.

'Sol, my gorgeous boy, I need an album like no other. You're the man. Impress me, babe. Turn out a few tunes that'll make Madonna wanna do murder.'

Sol looked at his dad. Dave was willing him to say yes.

'Oh, and I need the first one by Friday.'

Sol laughed and shook his head. She'd made that very easy indeed. 'I'm going away,' he said.

'What?' Dave's head was in his hands now.

'I'm getting out,' Sol said.

She stepped back and looked him up and down. 'What d'you mean, getting out?' There was a trace of a sneer on the crimson lips.

'I can't stand it, Sheba – I'm just a shell, my life's a sham.'

'Don't be ridiculous. You have everything anyone could want. And believe me – you can have twice that if you deliver a dozen great songs for me.'

'Exactly, and what's the point? It's all meaningless. Success, sex, money, music: it's all empty.'

Dave raised his head, like a phoenix from the ashes, and his eyes burned brightly. 'Music is not empty,' he stated. 'You should never say that. Music is the voice of God.'

'Well then, I've lost my hearing. I need to go and find it again.'

'You can't flee from yourself,' purred Sheba, 'wherever you go – there you are.'

'That's sweet. Where d'you get that line? Put that into one of your songs.'

'I got it in therapy.'

'Then get your therapist to write your new album.'

Sol turned, gave his dad a quick sincere smile and scrambled out of the room.

'Call me when you get back then.' He heard his old man shout.

'*If* I get back,' Sol muttered.

He just started walking. His rucksack had enough to keep him going for a day or so until he found something. He left everything else. No car. No responsibilities. No job. No future. Everything just went round and round and came to nothing, anyway. Why bother lugging a weight like that round with you?

Later, when Sheba and her hounds had gone, Dave King stared at the video clip of his son strumming a guitar at age eight. The film flickered and suddenly Sol was twice that, swaggering about in swimming shorts looking like a Greek hero. It took Dave back, not just to those early days as a father – but to his own youth.

Dave's early days. Very different to his son's. He remembered so well that day when Sam Prophet had strolled through the door, looking for the next big thing. Actually he'd not been there, he'd been out shovelling bovine excrement into a slurry truck. Boy, it had been a long time since he'd had to live with the stench of excreted grass on his clothes.

Conversion

Sol stood on the station platform and waited for a sign. For something to happen, something to point him in the direction of the next stage of his life. For a while he stared at the darkening sky overhead, then down at the hard cold tracks, wondering if that was the best place to head for. Oblivion. He shuffled to the edge of the platform, crossing the yellow safety line. Death had never appeared so sweet before, so perfect, so releasing. No more thinking, no more reasoning, no more restlessness and bedding women. No more pretence. It wasn't as if he was depressed, far from it, the idea of himself sprawled on those tracks brought a feeling of elation – the vision of his head split and his brains and blood seeping into the grime and the litter looked so good right now.

Then the phone rang. It was an old school friend, and astonishingly he was begging a favour. A favour that would save Sol's life. Sure he'd do it. He really needed to – there was no other choice ahead of him. He could still jump on the tracks later.

And there was Rhea too – maybe on the way he'd visit her. It was in the right direction. The train pulled up and he ran to the office to buy a ticket before it left. It was touch and go; the ticket clerk was slow and reluctant, a big man with a curtain of black hair shielding his eyes from the customers. But Sol willed him on and his eyes lasered silent pleading at him throughout the entire transaction, and somehow it was done and he bought the ticket and he was on the train. Relief, at last – the future was an unwritten page. He sat down at a table and started scribbling. He wrote the first thing that came to mind, and of course, for a guy who was on the run from a thousand women, it had to be a tribute to the wonders of sex. He didn't want to write it, right then he hated sex. It was the one thing that showed him up for the sham he was, but he couldn't escape it; like everything else he'd stuffed himself full and still found himself empty. He wrote and wrote and wrote. And then he scribbled about other things: it was as if skimming off the sensual surface of his life unearthed the deeper urges, the deeper regrets and desires. Once the defences started to tumble, they tumbled entirely.

Powerful rhetoric began to cut across his thinking and he looked up to see a ragged figure standing between the seats. A red-eyed straggle of a homeless guy had stepped out of nowhere, and here he was eloquently begging on the train, pleading with painful politeness as he waved his battered paper cup in Sol's direction. Sol sat mesmerised: the man's life was on the line as surely as if he had his head pressed to the tracks in front of the oncoming train. He had little to live for, but more desire or energy than Sol. He'd been a teacher, a headteacher, so his story went, then the housing crash had forced him out of his home, his family had given up on him and before he knew it he had no fixed abode, and with no fixed abode, no job. And now he travelled the line, begging as a way to survive. Sol was reaching for his wallet when the ticket collector arrived, and before he could pass on any crisp new notes the teacher was gone, leaving his empty cup rolling around on the carriage floor. Sol reached down and scooped it up: it wasn't empty, it had thirty-seven pence in the bottom. Thirty-seven pence the man would never see.

Two hours and a few adventures later, Sol sat in a restaurant, with a cold beer and a warm chicken pizza, a copy of *The Alchemist* on his left and the rucksack under his chair. He was starting to feel free – like Jules out of *Pulp Fiction* – walking the earth, following God and having adventures. Finding hope in another godless place, in another ordinary face.

On that short train ride he'd met a half a dozen real people who had no idea he was Dave King's son and didn't care anyway.

The guy who reached into his bag and gave Sol his copy of *The Alchemist*; the busker who'd been to China and was saving for India, who told him 'You can't see the Great Wall of China from the moon, but you can see the moon from the Great Wall.' The street vendor changing the world selling child sponsorships with every bit of her being. 'Do something small,' she insisted, shaking him by the shoulder, 'and change the world forever.' She claimed to have the knack of guessing your middle name and when she had recently guessed for one guy he had pledged to donate a huge whack of his inheritance. Sol asked if she got it in writing but she smiled and said he'd made his donation and a firm promise. They talked about the Dixie Chicks and street kids and Cambodia, and every time she talked about her plans some dam inside Sol cracked a little more. She seemed so clear-sighted: life's smoke hadn't clouded her vision yet.

It was years since anything like this had happened. When he was young and reckless Sol frequently absconded from school for a few hours, meandering wantonly through the streets of other peoples' lives. He'd forgotten that Life was out here. Amongst the card shops and fast food parlours. Oozing out of the dark corners and seeping across the street. Welling up in the restaurant waiters and the passing shoppers; in the homeless buskers and the shop assistants. Suddenly he had eyes to see and ears to hear and the world was crackling with the static of life.

He felt like he'd just woken up. He'd come out into the world with no agenda and suddenly his senses had stirred. It was like God had just stuck a big stick in his brain and rattled it around a bit. All those bits that were asleep got smacked about and started to react and spark and hum. Life buzzed through his head like electricity and for the first time in years he became conscious something was going on. The great beyond was closer than he ever thought: it had way more to do with regular life than random miracles.

Rhea

He stopped outside the school yard and stood watching the children hopscotching across the playground. He slowly became aware of the gathering crowd of parents around him, and realised he looked a little out of place in his rock'n'roll clothes.

'Dad!'

The kids flooded out of the gate, some limping shyly, bags trailing on the ground, others hurtling like rockets.

Only one of them stopped dead in her tracks.

'Rhea?'

Sol had a daughter. Rhea. A beautiful, wild, quirky, green-eyed angel.

And she was standing there, right in front of him, blinking wildly and saying: 'Daddy?'

It had been a while. A long time, in fact. Kids grew up so fast and you only had to be an absent father for a few weeks and they'd changed identity altogether. She recognised him though; he still had the same self-conscious rock-star persona.

He considered himself a bad father, mainly because he was never around and broke both their hearts whenever he left the beautiful shining little angel with her mother; yet still he never quite found it in him to spend more time with her. Family life seemed like a cage whilst bachelordom was an open range, an endless prairie of good beer, free women and ripe opportunity. There was no end and no limit. And no fathoming why it still left him feeling cut adrift, groping in the dark for some purpose and . . .

'Daddy!'

She threw herself at him, and because he was stooping to her level as she came, it knocked both of them backwards onto the pavement. She didn't care; other adults scattered as their bodies went skittling across the ground.

'Rhea, careful.'

'Daddy, I didn't know you were coming today.'

He glanced up to see a teacher hovering nearby, eyes narrow and trained on him. She relaxed as she recognised him, no mean achievement considering he turned up about as frequently as a tax rebate. The teacher nodded at him, he recalled her name and mouthed it back at her. She was short, blonde and not at all bad look . . .

'Daddy! Can we go to Robin Hood's?' Rhea was hanging onto his neck, pulling his head around as if it were a punch bag.

'Yes! OK! OK!'

He scooped her up and clawed her hands off his neck. 'What is Robin Hood's – a burger bar?'

It was an adventure playground. All swings and roundabouts. She tore around the place, ducking and diving and leaping out at him as he trailed behind like a weary basset hound on Prozac. He sort of knew what he was supposed to do in these kinds of situations: he just couldn't always bring himself to do it. Other dads excelled at chasing, tumbling and building castles out of the nearest natural substance, he could only stand back and wonder at their paternal ingenuity. His head was always away in other places . . .

He took his eyes off her for a split second to glance at a passing brunette and there was a sudden yell from the roundabout. She had spun off and cracked her knee on the floor.

He swooped in with all the deadly efficiency of a SWAT team and scooped her up. She was writhing about, gripping her knee and wailing.

'Oh Rhea, was it your funny bone, sweetie?' He hammed it up, 'your not-sure-whether-to-laugh-or-cry-bone?'

She pouted and giggled and frowned in quick succession. He rubbed her knee and quickly turned it into a tickling session. Rhea squealed and broke free and hurled herself at the swings. She tripped and injured her other knee, cried for two seconds then got up and carried on. Sol glanced across the park. The brunette was long gone.

Originally the whole idea of being a dad had set his head on fire with dreams and visions. An endless round of games with the fruit of his loins. A new kid off the block to impress. But with the onset of sleepless nights and putrid nappies, the increasing loss of evenings out and days off, the magic soon shrivelled and died, while the fruit of his loins did anything but shrivel. She developed in all directions, not least vocally, and before he knew it he was just another absent father who turned up when he felt like it and soothed the pain of both of them with trips to Burger King.

'Fancy a milkshake?' he yelled, after half an hour of the madness.

She looked up from the sandpit and nodded, her face a gritty, dusty smile.

Anything

'Daddy, if you could have anything, what would you have?'

'Anything?'

'Yeah.'

He chewed on his burger and thought for a while. 'I kind of already have everything,' he said.

'What d'you mean?'

'Well, granddad Dave is very rich, and he gave me a really good job.'

'You work for granddad?'

'Kind of – I'm what they call a talent scout.'

'Mike's brother is a scout, he wears a woggle.' She giggled at the sound of the word. 'Woggle woggle woggle!'

'I'm not that sort of a scout, more like a sort of agent.'

'A secret agent? Like the Incrudibles?'

'Incredibles. No, I look for good songs and great singers.'

'Am I great singer? I could be one day, couldn't I? I could go to granddad's house and sing something and he could play me on his big machine.'

He laughed. 'Rhea – you can be anything you want.'

'Where d'you find all the people and the songs?'

'Oh, here and there, I hear people singing in pubs and bars, bus queues, coffee shops. I'm always listening out.'

'Churches?'

'Maybe. Lots of rock'n'roll singers came out of church choirs.'

'What's rot'n'roll?'

'It's a kind of music, sweetie.'

'Daddy, you know in heaven?' Rhea said.

'Ye-e-es?' he said cautiously.

'We'll be able to see God, won't we?

'Er . . . ye-e-e-e-es.'

'Goodie, 'cause then we won't have to pretend, will we?'

'Ah, no I suppose not.'

'Do you say prayers, Daddy?'

'Yeah, but don't tell anybody.'

'Why not?'

He wasn't sure now that she asked. 'I guess people just don't talk about it very much. You know,' he snapped his fingers, 'you've reminded me about something I'd forgotten. I had a dream once about having everything I wanted. It was when I was quite young. I dreamt I met God.'

Rhea's eyes popped. 'God? What did he look like? Was he big? Did he have a beard like Uncle Nathan?'

'Not sure, he kind of looked like a person.'

'A boy or a girl?'

'A man, I think. He took me for a walk and said I could have anything I wanted. So you know what I asked for?'

'A computer?'

'No, darling, I said I wanted to be really clever. So I could work things out, and he said, good answer, that'll bring you lots of other good things.'

Rhea went quiet. She put down her milkshake and looked at her plate. 'Daddy?'

'Yeah?'

'You know what I'd ask for if I met God?'

He shook his head and glanced around at the other single parents child-minding in the restaurant.

'You.'

He turned back and blinked at her. 'Me?'

'You and Mummy living together with me. All of us together.'

Now they both fell silent. Rhea pushed food around her plate, Sol shuffled the excuses around his head.

'When I grow up I don't want to get married. I'm going to live with Ruth and Joel and Esther and Daniel. And you and Mummy too. We're all going to live together. None of us are going to get married. It'll be fun.' A pause for breath then, 'Do you love Mummy?'

'Yes, of course.'

'Then why don't you live with her?'

There was no easy way to answer this. 'I think . . . I'm a bit selfish, Rhea, I like being able to run around and do what I want.'

'We could all run around together, I like doing that.'

'I know you do, darling, I know . . .'

'Mummy likes doing that.'

'Mummy likes doing what? What the hell's going on?'

They looked up. Sol's wife was standing over them, one hand on Rhea, the other clenched in a small fist. He noticed she was still wearing the ring. They had never officially split.

'Hi, gorgeous.'

She wasn't flattered. 'Sol! You . . . you can't do this! I thought she'd been abducted or something. You don't just come and take her out of school.'

Her eyes were boring right into him. This wasn't just about Rhea, this was about everything that had ever gone wrong between them.

'Well, you weren't there. I'd have asked you if you'd been there with her.'

'I'm always there with her! I was stuck in traffic.'
'Daddy's here, Mummy.'
'I can see, darling. Come on, let's go home. You frightened the life out of me.'
'Can Daddy come with us?'
She looked at him as if to say, not a hope in hell.
He went with them.

She put on the soundtrack to *The Lion King* to break the silence in the car.

'How did you know where we'd be?' he asked.

'You're predictable,' she said, her lips barely parting to let the words escape.

'We were just discussing what we might do if we could have anything,' he said, forcing a bright smile.

'I'd have Daddy back,' chirped Rhea and she went straight into the chorus of 'Can you feel the love tonight?'

'I wouldn't,' his wife muttered, but not loud enough for Rhea to catch. 'What are you doing round here anyway? Someone opened a new gambling casino? Or is it some new tart you're checking out for your dad?'

'Believe it or not, I'm on an errand of mercy.'

And he told her about Jake, and the audition with Leah. He was still talking when they pulled up outside her house. It was in a nice part of town: she could never accuse Sol of withholding funds from his estranged family. Money couldn't buy them love, but it got a whole lot of other things.

'You going to come in then?' she said, her voice uninviting.

He shrugged, but Rhea was already clambering over him and pulling at his clothes.

'Daddy, come in, I've got my new bedroom to show you.'

Anything

It was pink. Totally pink. She had a new bunk bed with everything a girl could ever want built into the unit underneath. Including a kitchen sink. She poured him tea and sliced up plastic pizza while he sat on the bunk holding a Barbie in a tutu. The doll was in the tutu, not him. He lay back and was just starting to doze when he heard a familiar voice downstairs. He sat bolt upright, almost fell off the bed and scrambled downstairs, Rhea close on his heels.

It was Tamar. She was standing in the kitchen supping tea from a mug that said . . . 'She looked at him with a bemused smirk.' Which she promptly did.

'You two know each other?'

'Daddy, look! I can hop backwards. Look! Watch me! And I can do a big jump on the sofa. Come on. Let me show you. Daddy, come on, Daddy, come on.'

'I'll be back,' he said and Tamar mouthed, 'Promises, promises.'

Half an hour later as Rhea was parading up and down the hall in her pyjamas and her daddy's shoes, Sol ventured back into the kitchen. Tamar and his wife were tucking into pasta and green salad. The plates were overshadowed by two monstrous glasses of red wine.

'I figured you wouldn't want to eat, seeing as you'd just dined out. Cheeseburger, wasn't it?' his wife said, without looking at him.

'How d'you two know each other?' he asked. 'And d'you have any beer?'

'Through Men-haters Anonymous. And yes, I do, why?'

Sol shrugged and cracked a sheepish frown. 'Please may I have one? I promise I'll put the loo seat down if I need to use it afterwards.'

Tamar laughed. His wife shook her head. 'Sol, what are you doing here? You know you're not supposed to just wash up like a piece of driftwood. It's unsettling.'

'I told you, I'm helping someone, and I'm sort of trying to find myself.'

Both women laughed now.

'Well, good luck with that,' said Tamar and they raised their glasses and clinked them.

Sol ignored their mocking. 'Tamar,' he said, 'you know that guy across the road from you?'

'Cain?'

'Yeah. You know his sister's missing?'

Tamar shrugged.

'Can you do me a favour? Can you find out if he's got a copy of *Brief Encounter*?'

'I had a friend who used to run a lingerie shop called that,' said his wife.

'Yes, yes,' Sol said wearily. 'I've heard it. Many times.'

'Sol. You're not still going on about that film, are you?' Tamar said. 'Don't worry. I don't wanna watch it. In fact, I'm seriously starting to hate the movie.'

'Tamar, please just ask him. It's important. I think he knows something about his sister. When I showed him that black leather book he was cagey about it – it made him jumpy. It was her Bible.'

'I read some of that book,' said Tamar. 'You know, there's a lot in there about women. It says if a man seduces a woman he has to marry her. Did you know that, Sol?'

His wife frowned. 'That won't work for Sol, polygamy's illegal in this country.'

'Whatever,' said Sol. 'The point here is – I don't trust him – Cain, I mean, he's weird.'

'All right, don't keep on about him . . .'

'I'll come see you in a couple of days . . .'

Tamar raised her eyebrows, his wife pursed her lips and shook her head.

'I don't wanna know,' she said, 'whatever you two get up to in that dark country pub, I just don't wanna know . . .'

'Daddy, I know what infinity plus infinity is.'

They all looked over to the doorway. Rhea was standing there with a giant panda on her head.

'It's one thousand.'

Normal

As the women finished their meal Sol put Rhea to bed, which included watching a chunk of *Flushed Away* on Mummy's laptop, both of them sitting in beanbag chairs on the landing and sucking on carrot sticks. It was supposed to take ten minutes but in fact stretched to forty. Two stories and three cuddles later and Rhea was finally in bed.

Sol flopped down on a chair in the kitchen and took a swig of warm beer.

'I'm exhausted,' he said.

'Welcome to the real world, honey,' his wife replied.

Tamar left soon after that and they suddenly found themselves alone and making eyes at one another across a crowded kitchen table.

Sol's wife had the widest smile in the world: he could resist anything except that smile. Maybe it was the wine, maybe she'd had a hard day, maybe she was just lonely. But she unleashed it on him now.

'So – how's the world of rock'n'roll?' she asked.

He shrugged. 'OK. Empty right now, if I'm honest.'

'That's 'cause you don't have me in it,' she said and Sol nodded.

'Why did we split up again?' he asked.

''Cause you're a philanderer,' she said, and she handed him a fresh beer.

'So why are you trying to get me drunk?' he asked.

'It's been a while – and why should everyone else have a piece of you when I can't?'

He sighed. 'I've got to be honest, I'm a mess right now.'

She knocked back the end of her wine and snorted a laugh. 'I always knew that,' she said. 'That was always very obvious.'

He stared at her, that face he knew so well, that smile, those astute, searching eyes. He said nothing, he just kept staring and falling deeper into her, and he realised what he'd been missing with all those one-night stands. Right there and then, with a couple of beers inside him, and their daughter peaceful and sleeping above their heads, he could have sat and stared forever.

'It would never work,' she said eventually. 'You don't care enough.'

He blinked and tore himself from the trance. 'What d'you mean?'

'I mean you love the poetry of all this, right now you recall everything that was good, but the moment you have to face everything that was bad – you'll be off. I love you Sol, I won't stop loving you, but you gotta love me too. And you gotta love normal life, and having a wife and child and shopping and mess and diarrhoea and vomit and nits and no time to listen to your music or watch your precious DVDs. That's the full package. You gotta love it all.'

'You're too honest, you always were.'

'Better than being too dishonest,' she said with feeling.

'All men are liars,' he said.

'Yeah, but some more than others.'

He didn't know what to say to that, so he went back to ogling her, and it worked, before too long they kissed, gently at first, very gently, then harder and longer and the taste of her lips made his heart race and his head swim.

'Don't break anything,' she hissed as they shoved things off the kitchen table and wrestled with each other's clothes.

'Mummy.'

They froze, too many clothes hanging undone.

'Yes, darling,' she turned away, hitched straps and fastened buttons, then turned back.

'I feel sick . . .'

And to prove it Rhea vomited on the kitchen floor. She was so fast that little splashes rose up and dotted Sol's shoes.

His wife scooped up Rhea and ran to the bathroom with her, yelling, 'Clean that up will you?' as she went.

She was right, Sol didn't love normal life. He didn't love it at all.

The next morning Sol awoke with feet pounding his groin. It hurt.

Sol yelled. He didn't mean to: had he not been woken up by pain in his nether regions, had he spent the last few years living with this, he would not have done it. But he wasn't used to it. He was used to waking up with older females who did not use that trick to get your attention.

So he yelled, and Rhea screamed and it took a while and some cuddling to calm her down. When Sol looked at the clock, it said 6.45 am.

'Daddy, Daddy, come on, let's play aeroplanes.'

'What?'

'Come downstairs and you lie on the sofa and put your feet in the air and I balance on them.'

He wasn't used to this. It was still dark out there. The clock still said 6.45. 6.45 am. didn't exist in his world.

'Come on Daddy.'

She was pulling on his right leg, yanking it from under the covers of the spare bed and bending it like a pipe cleaner in the wrong direction.

'Ow!'

'Come on, it's morning!'

Somehow he made it downstairs and found himself splattered across the sofa, legs in the air with Rhea lying flat on his upturned feet, soaring like a bird and roaring like a jet engine.

'That's it, now push me up. Push me up! I won't fall . . . This is really fun, Dad. Higher! Higher! I won't fall . . .'

She fell, and Sol ended up yelling again. There were more tears and this time it took a bowl of Coco Pops to calm everything down. By the time she was installed in front of kids' TV and he could safely return to bed, he was worn ragged.

He wasn't thinking straight and crawled into his old double bed. His wife was somehow still half asleep; she rolled over and curled her body round his as he sneaked in.

'Well done, Superman,' she muttered, and promptly fell asleep around him.

Two hours later and he was heading off, moving out of his old life and back on the hunt for Abby and himself. Rhea gave him an extremely long hug as he stood on the doorstep.

'I promise I'll be back soon,' he said.

'Wait here,' she said and she suddenly ran inside.

'She bought you a present,' his wife whispered.

'Look, Daddy!'

Rhea's eyes were wide, her broad smile lighting up her face like a firework. She proudly held up a huge orange bundle – it turned out to be a sweatshirt picked out just for him. Sol unravelled it and held it up.

'It says you're the daddy!' Rhea said, eyes gleaming. It did too.

'I'm the daddy,' Sol read out loud.

'Just in case you ever forget,' his wife said with a wink, 'and so she can recognise you on the rare occasions your paths cross. Oh! And I almost forgot . . .'

She disappeared and left Rhea on the doorstep with him.

Sol scooped her up and swung her round in his arms until she squealed.

'Daddy,' she said, as he slowed up, 'you're my favourite.'

'Favourite what?'

'Daddy.'

He stopped swirling her. 'Have . . . have there been a lot of other . . . daddies here for you?'

'They're all nice. One of them's really funny. He does jokes all the time. But I love you, Daddy.'

'I love you sweetie,' he said and he hugged her tightly again.

His wife reappeared. 'Here we go. I've been meaning to send them back to you. Sorry, I've had them ages.' She handed him two DVDs.

'*Hitch*! I wondered where this was.'

'Actually it's not *Hitch*. You'll have to keep looking. It's *Psycho*. You gotta get that collection sorted out. I didn't bother with *Lord of the Rings* in the end – life's too short.'

'Maybe you could come over and . . . help me sort my DVDs some time,' he said hopefully.

'No . . . but I'll come over and watch *Hitch* with you.'

He left the house and that's when the penny dropped. His wife, this person he'd spent so much of his time on, so much affection and energy, this girl who had once sweated blood in her own little corner of Gethsemane to bring his child into being, had become just another woman in his life, a convenient guardian for his precious daughter.

'Oi! Keep in touch won't you?' she called as he made his way up the road. There was something wistful, something unfinished in her call to him. Sol turned and glanced back. She was standing in the doorway, cuddling Rhea in her arms. 'Don't be a stranger.'

It made him wonder whether the day would come when the definition of a father might well be just that – someone who 'kept in touch'.

'I mean it,' she shouted again, 'keep in touch.'

He nodded and wondered how much *touch* they might manage in the years ahead. Maybe the kitchen table would prove successful one day.

As he walked Sol ran a hand through his hair and realised something serious. He needed a cut. Doing something new would make him feel better, make him feel like he was starting over. He hurried across the road, narrowly missing two kids on bikes as he went, then he realised he was going the wrong way, checked himself, spun round and strode back into town. He found the nearest salon and went in. As he sat inside waiting the light dawned. He grabbed *The Lord of the Rings* and flipped the case open. There it was: his copy of *Brief Encounter*.

Wrestling

Mosher looked up from his place on the floor amongst the mess of cables. 'Someone was looking for you last night,' he said as Jake shuffled in.

'Someone? Who?' Jake replied

'Some bird,' said Mosher. 'Came asking after you'd gone. Late last night. I was just replacing the hard drives in the . . .'

'I don't care about the hard drives,' said Jake, terror lurking behind his eyes, 'What did she look like?'

Mosher shrugged and shoved hair out of his face. 'Red hair. Legs. Arms. And all the usual woman bits. Not young. Not bad though.'

'Red hair?'

'Think so, you know these damn hard drives are always failing, we gotta change our supplier, one day it'll go on air and then you'll be back to playing all that viral stuff.'

'Vinyl.'

'Whatever.'

Jake wasn't listening: if his mother was looking for him and could find him here, then so could Esau.

Jake set up for the show but was rattled, and in a bad mood, and when he felt like this he was liable to say plenty he might regret. He wasn't long into the show before the texts were hailing down on him like a storm of wasteful snipers' bullets.

'I'm in trouble again, average punters out there,' he told the public. 'After playing the Illiterati's new single "Can't spell my own name" and then announcing it was dedicated to today's youth I've caused an outcry. You are not happy. Apparently there are dozens of young guns out there who can actually spell your own names. Well – that's dandy. Just brilliant! Certainly bodes well for the future then, doesn't it? Here's Manfred Mann and the kind of song that dreams are made of, albeit very weird dreams induced by something external becoming illegally internal, "Blinded by the light".'

It was a dilemma for him, this foaming at the mouth business, because he often spoke out more truth when he was angry. Yet it wasn't therapeutic: it just left him feeling bad.

He glanced at the playlist, Sixpence short of a fruitcake were due up next with their cover of 'Jeans on'. He scowled and swapped it for the Imagineers and 'Making up time'. The phone rang.

Jake didn't feel like talking to any angry teenagers so he left it. Eventually it stopped. He told another story and put on Dylan and the Dead. The phone rang again. He stared at it, braced himself and eventually took the call.

'You're gonna die.'

'We're all gonna die, mate.'

'Yeah, but you sooner than most.'

'Look, all I said was . . .'

'It's not what you said, it's what you did.'

'What? Who is this? I'm not in the mood to . . .'

'I'm coming for you.'

'Who the hell are you?

'You know.'

'What do you mean?

'You thought you could take the money and run and live happily ever after. Well forget that for a tin of maggots, mate. You owe me big time – that's my money you spent on that run-down God spot you bought . . .'

'How d'you know about . . . ?'

'And there's an old man dying 'cause of you. You should be coughing up blood – not him.'

'Esau?'

A laugh on the other end of the line. 'As far as you're concerned – I'm God and it's time for retribution. This prodigal ain't gonna come home to a fatted calf – he'll be the one roasting. So you'd better watch your back, little runaway – 'cause from now on – you're not safe. Anywhere. I'll be waiting.'

'Listen mate, you're not God and I'm not . . .'

Too late: there was no one listening at the other end. His brother had gone.

Phil Oakey

'I want a Human League.'

The hairdresser behind him frowned. She stared at him in the mirror and adjusted the towel round his neck. Sol realised she looked about fifteen.

'How old are you?' he asked.

'Twenty. Why?' She spoke as if her two decades had not lived up to expectation.

'What are you looking forward to?'

She curled her lip and twisted the ends of her ponytail.

'The weekend,' she said.

'Is that all?'

'I'm going to see Westlife. I've been waiting for months. It'll be a right laugh.' She started humming 'You raise me up' then said, 'What about you then? What are you gonna do?'

'Get a haircut and then . . .' he thought for a moment. 'Either travel the world or . . . kill myself.'

She looked as if someone had just ripped up her Westlife ticket.

He laughed. 'Don't worry – I'm not really suicidal – just bored. That's why I want a Human League.'

The girl ran her fingers through his hair; her nails were pink and flecked with glitter.

'Is that like a political party?'

'The Human League?'

'My brother's into politics,' she said. 'Reckons he'll be Prime Minister one day. Well, my dad reckons he will, anyway.'

'Phil Oakey.'

She stared again and stopped ruffling his hair.

'That's the guy I was trying to think of: lead singer with the Human League. He had one side long, the other short. That's what I want.'

She frowned. 'One side long and the other short. That'll look stupid.'

'Yep. And right now that's how I feel. Screwed up. Split down the middle. It'll be symbolic – a symbolic haircut. At war with itself. Yep. I'll have a Phil Oakey.'

Rach was sitting on the brow of the hill outside The Ladder. She turned to look at him. She'd cleaned up. It was astonishing. Her hair was clean and shone like bronze. Her face was smooth and there was colour in her cheeks.

She smiled at him, jumped up and swung her bag towards him. Only it wasn't a bag. It was a fence post and somehow she had the strength to launch it at him. Jake dodged and the wood tore against his cheek as he moved. He heard a crash and turned to see the post shattering the windscreen of a nearby four-by-four.

'Rach! What are you doing?'

She smiled and pushed him backwards, hard enough to knock the breath out of him. He lost his footing and fell on his back and the next thing he knew she was swinging her foot at his head. At the last minute he grabbed it and twisted her ankle. There was a crunch and she yelped. And Jake knew. It was happening again. The dream. His life was locked inside it and here it was again. He tried to wake, strained to escape, but he had no power for that. All he could do was duck and dive and do his best to stay alive. Rach was incredibly strong in dreamworld, and it was exhausting.

Jake woke, covered in sweat. When would it end? Was he going mad? Last night it had been Leah and the night before that his old dad. It was as if the dream was on repeat play. Esau's phone call had freaked him, and though no one had yet contacted him at the chapel, he knew it couldn't be long. If he ever saw his brother again he'd be pulped. No contest. They'd parted on a death threat, and it wasn't issued by Jake. Somewhere inside him, Jake knew that the end was inevitable. It was only a matter of time.

Raised by wolves

He rubbed his eyes and rolled over. Leah was sitting up in the other bed, running her hand though her hair. They never shared a bed: Jake was too restless and Leah slept too lightly. She was on the phone, that must have been the jangling that had dragged Jake from the nightmare. He was grateful for it.

'It's for you,' said Leah, coming over and kissing him lightly on the cheek as she passed the phone. 'Some chick called Rebekah. You'd better not be two-timing me.'

And she slipped out of the room.

'Mum? What . . . how d'you find me? They said you came to the station.'

The voice on the other end sounded quieter and more hesitant than he remembered. He'd always been close to his mother. Much closer than the fractured relationship with his old man.

'Your dad's very sick, Jake. He's had a stroke.'

'What? When?'

'While you've been away. A month ago. I've been doing all I can to track you down.'

'Does Esau know?'

'Of course. He was with your father when it happened.'

'No, does he know you've found me?'

'Jake! Your dad.'

'Sorry . . . I . . .'

'When are you coming home?'

Jake shrugged and shook his head. No way, no way. Fortunately his mum couldn't see. 'Soon,' he said, and he hung up.

Leah walked back in, drink in hand. 'Who's this Rebekah then?'

'My mum.'

'Oh, so you do have family then? I was beginning to think you were raised by wolves.'

'No. It just felt like it sometimes.'

'You never talk about them – what's your mum like?'

'She's got red hair.'

'Oh well, that tells me everything.' Leah started daubing crimson varnish on her toenails. 'Rach's got red hair,' she said.

'I know . . .' he paused and flinched. She twisted her head sharply to look at him. He scrambled on, desperately searching for a loophole. 'I mean . . . I remember that because . . . you showed me a picture.'

'Did I?'

'Yeah. Definitely.'

'Don't remember.' She went back to her toes. 'What about brothers and sisters? Got any?'

'A brother.'

'I wanna meet him.'

'No, you don't.'

'Yes, I do.'

'No, you don't.'

'Why not?'

'He'd kill you.'

'You should dye your hair.'

'What?'

Leah always did this – just when they started to talk about something real she'd be off into Neverland, chasing stardust and dreaming up ludicrous schemes.

'You'd look good with blonde hair – spiky, fiery red tips. I'll do it for you. Be good for your radio image.'

'No one sees you on the radio.'

'Shame. 'Cause they'll want to now. Come on.'

'Now?'

'Now.'

'But we haven't got any bleach.'

She laughed derisively. 'A girl always has a bottle of bleach.'

While Jake sat with a plastic bag on his head, waiting for the bleach to take hold, Leah picked up the black book.

'I found you in here,' she said, holding it up.

Jake look confused. 'Me?'

'Yeah and me. It's weird. This bloke does a runner from his family and guess what? Sees a load of angels going up and down a ladder – in a place called – wait for this – Bethel! Spooky, eh? And then he meets this gorgeous girl and falls for her . . .' she scowled, 'unfortunately called Rachel.' She spat the last word out. 'But shock horror – she has a sister called, get this, Leah, and Leah has beautiful eyes. And she gives him six kids. Six! So obviously she was good in bed. Actually it's kind of sad because every time she has a kid she says, "Maybe now Jake'll love me" – 'cause she knows he secretly loves Rachel – yeah, like that would ever happen. But what do you think Jake – would you love me if I gave you six kids?'

Jake took the book and read the paragraph she'd marked. It sent shivers down his spine.

That night of leaving was burned deep into Jake's being, as surely as if he'd had the whole story tattooed across his chest. His old man had lost his sight: it had been fading for years and now it had reached the point that either twin could stand in front of him and he'd not know which it was.

'Jake!' Earlier in the day Rebekah had called him outside, well away from everyone else.

'Your dad's plotting. I can tell, he's been stewing on something for days, he's sent your brother out for some fresh meat. Not any old meat, his favourite butcher. That'll take a while. I'll cook some food instead – you take it to him, you can do a passable impression of your brother . . .'

'I can't do a passable impression of Esau . . .'

'Shut up. Do it. It'll be worth your while . . . trust me . . .'

And there he was in front of his dad, his frail, blind, old dad, getting vital information about the whereabouts of a certain safe deposit box containing a bagful of diamonds that held the future: a future that Jake was gonna steal from his brother.

And so he took the information and, like the prodigal, he ran, not daring to look back, on his way to freedom and a small fortune. That first night he slept in a cheap guest house, somewhere they'd never find him, in a room with a nicotine-stained carpet, chintz curtains and mildewed wallpaper.

Then the next day he caught a bus and found the bank his father had visited on the day of their birth. A day of hope for the future, before life had been sullied by the reality of family feuding and jealous brotherhood.

'See? Just like you!' said Leah with a knowing smile. 'Now let's take that bag off and have a look at that blond hair.'

Close to home

'Tonight, I wanna do what I always do, tell you a story,' Jake shifted in his seat and adjusted the mic a little. The words weren't coming easy this show. He glanced down at the little black book in front of him. He'd borrowed it off Leah before slipping out to work with his new fiery blond look. 'I wanna tell you a story about two brothers. Two guys who hated each other. One enough to steal, the other enough to kill. The world's full of families who are collapsing, well, here's another for you. The mother and little brother in the red corner, Dad and the older lad in the blue. And the gloves are off. Let's call the boys Jon and Ed. It's easier. Jon is scared of Ed, but knows he can outwit him. So he does, he sets up a scam to extricate funds from their old man's account and takes off with the loot. Pretty much all of it. You see, Jon's spent his life growing up in the shadow of Ed. Ed is Dad's favourite – a real hunter-gatherer type. Jon is cool, wily, a genius-on-his-feet kind of guy. His mother's boy.' Jake winced as he said this. 'So Ed rebels, shacks up with all the wrong women, deliberately goes out of his way to punish his parents for what's happened. He's ended up broke and sidelined. And he issues a threat. If he ever sees Jon again – he'll kill him.' He paused, lifted his bottle of water and swigged it back, his hands shook a little and his throat had been drier than usual. He licked the excess drops from his lips and went on. 'So Jon is on the run now. Looking for a safe place to hide.

'And he meets two sisters, Lara and Ruth. Ruth is beautiful and runaway Jon wants to marry her, but he's tricked – the trickster is tricked by his new father-in-law, and he ends up with Lara. Lara knows Jon doesn't love her, but she tries to win his love, tries to give him sex and children to win him over. But Jon's heart is elsewhere, he's given it to Lara's sister, and try as she might, Lara can't get it back. You know the ending to all this? Me neither. All I know is life is messy and no amount of radio banter can sort it out. If you have any advice, average punters, feel free to email it in. My life hangs by a thread and the best answer gets a free Radio Sunshine mug and a bumper sticker. Oh and a copy of the album of the week. *Waking Sleeping Dogs* by Slade. Always useful as a trendy coaster . . .'

He instantly regretted telling the story, it was all too close to home, and the characters might have been straight out of the little black book but they were people out of his own life too. And that was dangerous. His mother had obviously found him on the airwaves: not his old man, the brittle old stick was never a radio guy. And Esau had. It was the height of stupidity to run a radio show when you were trying to remain lost and anonymous.

'Sol, it's Jake, you still on for the show? You won't be disappointed, mate. Be good to catch up about the old times too. Call me when you get here.'

There hadn't really been old times, just two boys in the same school, but answerphones made you say stupid things. Jake hung up, and drove back to the Ladder. It was late evening now. He went inside, bought two drinks and took them back out. Then he set down his rucksack and sat on the brow of the hill soaking up the wonder of the view. It was what he needed. He'd almost given up waiting when he saw the slight figure dawdling towards him through the trees.

She flopped down on the grass, he handed her the drink and she leant back on her elbows and sighed.

'Ever heard of the Tiger Trees?' she said. 'Great little band from the sixties. I forgot about them till last night. Then I dreamt I was at a gig they were playing.' She shut her eyes and gave a little smile. 'You should check them out for your show.'

'Rach, I got a present for you, I figured you'd like it.'

He handed her the black book. The mist had come down as they sat there.

'It's seen a bit of life but then so have you, I guess,'

She shrugged. 'Thanks, nicest thing you've ever said to me.'

She was pleased though, he could see that. She sat there flicking the pages, stopping every so often to pore over one, like a child with a new picture book. His heart melted a little.

'Rach,' he whispered, 'can I kiss you?'

She recoiled, horror in her eyes.

'No way! Just 'cause you gave me a Bible it doesn't give you access to my underwear.'

He shook his head. 'It's not like that. I love you, Rach.'

'Yeah, right. No. No, you can't kiss me. And it's always *like that* with men.' She said *men* as if it was an expletive.

Jake nodded sadly and stood up. 'I'll just say goodbye then. Won't be round here again, Rach. I've loved these nights with you – but I've got to go.'

She noticed his rucksack for the first time. 'You really are going, aren't you?'

He nodded, kissed his fingers and pressed them gently against her cheek. Surprisingly she didn't pull away, in fact, for a moment, she pressed her face against his skin.

'I've loved them too,' she said suddenly and sadly, 'these nights I mean.' She was staring right at him. 'No bloke ever treated me like you before.'

She gave him a shy smile and he nodded. He didn't know what else to do. He loved her but he had to go.

'Bye Rach,' he said and he started to walk off into the mist. She didn't follow. He looked back and pointed at the book. 'Careful with that, you might find yourself in there.'

She smiled. 'I'll be disappointed if I don't,' she said and she began studying the delicate pages again.

Jake went home and crept into bed. Leah was already tucked up, cuddling her Buffy the Vampire Slayer hot water bottle. Jake lay awake for a long time and watched the walls closing in.

Blood and hate

The guy had blood on his knuckles and hate etched in his eyes.

He grabbed Jake by the collar and pulled him down a side alley. It was incredibly quiet, way too quiet for Jake's good.

'I'm gonna kill you.'

'I've got money – lots of it.'

'I'm not after your money – day after day you walk past me and you never give me a second glance.'

'Why should I?'

'Because I'm human.'

'Look, I don't know what you're talking about . . .'

'Yes, you do.'

The guy's fist tightened on Jake's neck, flecks of his discoloured spit were landing on his face at regular intervals. He did his best not to flinch but he could feel spots on his lips.

'I've watched you, I've seen the way you treat people. You should think again.'

'I . . . really don't get this.'

The guy spun him round and slammed him hard against the far wall. Jake's face was inches from a rusting spike that protruded from the filthy brickwork, any closer and it would have pierced his eye socket.

'You're like all the rest. Head up your own backside. What's the view like up there?'

'Right now – dark. Look, whatever you want . . .'

'It's not about what I want, it's what you want. What do you want? Really? What do you want? Do you want anything that will last?'

'Who are you?'

'I told you, someone who's waiting for your attention.'

'Well, you got it now.'

'No, I haven't. 'Cause right now all you're thinking is, I wanna be safe, I want out of here. I want to get this nutter off my back, preferably with as little spare cash and inconvenience as possible. That's not what I call attention.'

'Look mate . . . I know nothing about you.'

'Exactly. The question is – do you wanna find out? Or do you wanna just keep going on your own sweet, stagnant way?'

Jake looked him squarely in the face. It was a history of violence, a road map of cuts and bruises. He couldn't help but be honest.

'I'm not sure. I don't even believe this is happening. I don't want you in my life. I want this to be over.'

The guy gave him a searing stare, his eyes burning right into Jake's soul. Then he smiled. Not sadistically, just a smile. And he let Jake go.

'There you go. A bit of honesty. That's worth something.'

And he reached inside his coat and pulled out a wad of notes. They were crisp and clean and every one a fifty.

'I don't need your money, mate.'

'I know, I'm just showing you I don't need yours.'

And he shoved the pile into Jake's hand.

'You'll never be rid of me. So work out what you really want.'

Then the guy pulled a razor from his hand and sliced it across his own wrist.

'What are you doing? What are you doing? No!'

It was too late, the blood was bursting from his artery like the blast from a deluxe water rifle, the crimson jet shot Jake in the chest, so it looked as if they were both dying.

'My clothes . . . I don't know you! Why are you doing this? . . . Look at the mess . . . Is this some kind of death-wish?'

The guy gave a weak grin. '*No, it's a lifewish*,' he said and he collapsed at Jake's feet, dousing his socks in a river of red.

There was a clatter and Jake saw the razor land in the growing puddle. Instinctively he scooped it up. His hands were doused in the other guy's life.

'This can't be happening, this can't be happening . . .'

In his dreams friends and strangers attacked him and beat him up and wrestled him to the floor. They didn't take a razor and bleed all over him. He fished in his pocket for his mobile; of course it was the wrong pocket and he ended up getting blood everywhere before he'd located the phone.

'There's a man dying here. I want the hospital! An ambulance! Get me someone who can keep him alive . . .'

He was still talking when he heard steps and turned to see the cops. Two juveniles in blue uniforms with sticks and torches. Where were they two minutes back? He half expected them to say, 'Ello? What's going on here then?'

But they didn't.

Before he knew it they'd clamped a jacket around the leaking wrist and radioed for backup. Jake fell back against the wall, turned his head and threw up.

'Did you know this man?' one of them asked.

Jake spat and shook his head.

'Esau Canaan,' the cop said, studying a card in his hand. 'His name's Esau Canaan.'

Jake stared at the bloodless face cradled in the policeman's pink fingers.

'What? Esau . . . but . . .'

His brother looked up at him, smiled a weak smile, then passed out. Jake lifted his hand to wipe his mouth and realised he was smearing spit across a handful of fifty pound notes.

'Was he after that money?' the cop said.

Jake froze, then gave the faintest of nods.

'And the blade? The razor?'

They both glanced down at the weapon hanging down by Jake's leg, still clutched in his fist.

'I . . . I pulled it off him in the struggle . . .' Jake said.

'Are you injured?'

Jake weighed up the situation and made the wrong decision. He hid his hand behind his leg and slid his fingers across the blade. Twice. He did his best not to wince. 'Oh . . . yeah . . . it must have happened during the struggle.'

He lifted his hand and saw blood oozing from the cuts.

'We'll get you sorted.'

The ambulance came and Jake climbed inside while they carried the body on board. He sat and stared at the calm, bloodless face on the trolley opposite him. Jake started to count the number of lies he'd rattled out in the last minutes. The list was ugly. He looked at the fistful of bloody cash in his fingers and started counting that.

There were hundred of notes. Thousands of pounds. Blood money. The counting made his head swim, and before he knew it, he was falling into a deep sleep.

Looking after number one

Jake woke up. And the nightmare was over. Another one. Another night of wrestling, with nothing to show for it but sweat and twisted memories. But it had not been like this before: the dreams had never featured his brother.

Why was this happening to him? Why the persistent nightmares? He wasn't a bad person. He'd just done what any insecure sibling might do. OK, so he'd cheated his family but he wasn't a murderer or a rapist or an arsonist. He didn't even wait for red bills before paying up. Sure, he broke the speed limit, but then most people did, and it indicated his desire to keep ahead of others. He always paid the speeding fines and went to the workshops to avoid points on his licence. As he wandered out of the chapel that morning and down towards Mo Mountain, nursing an extra strong espresso, he caught the strains of the Boomtown Rats on the radio; Bob Geldof yelling at him from the open bathroom window about looking after number one. Was this his great crime? If it was, then why weren't the alleyways clogged with people being mugged by suicidal philanthropists?

Everyone looked after number one, didn't they? It was the old survival instinct. But he couldn't go on like this. Something had to be done.

His mobile rang. It was Sol. He was in town to do the interview. He sounded in good form. He was at the station: they agreed to meet up and Jake jumped in his car.

'Nice hair.' Sol said.

Jake nodded. 'I could say the same,' he muttered, a little in awe of his old schoolmate.

'Your own radio show then?' Sol looked impressed.

Jake shrugged. 'Hardly Radio One,' he said, 'just a good solid show so I can pontificate about good music.'

They were understandably wary of each other: they'd spent time at the same school but Sol was a good two years older, and two years at school was a lifetime. Jake had watched the other guy from a respectful distance. Admiring his style, his wit, and, most of all, his ability to pick up girls.

Leah was waiting in the studio. Mosher had set up her guitar and plumbed it into the system. One of the bosses had put in an unexpected appearance and was lurking like a sharp-suited wolf in the shadows. Jake was nervous: he'd abandoned too many playlists lately. In just a few seconds he saw the whole scenario in his head, Leah would play badly, Sol would be disgusted, Jake would be out of work.

'Hi gorgeous, this is Sol,' Jake said as they slipped into studio one. 'We go back a long way.'

He and Sol, knowing they didn't, looked at each other and laughed. Leah was nervous and showed it. Sol offered her his hand.

'Don't worry about me,' he said, 'my old man's the celebrity. I don't mix with the great and the good, I just help other people do that.'

She smiled and strummed her guitar.

'How many songs d'you want to do?' Jake asked, one eye on the lurking executive beyond the glass.

'Three. Is that OK? How many do they normally do?'

'Three's fine, strum something will you, and sing into that mic.'

Her voice sounded terrible. Sol slipped out for a bottle of water for her. On the way he shook hands with the studio boss and smiled his charming smile. Jake watched them chatting and saw the boss's eyebrows rise a mile when he learnt Sol's name. Jake smiled to himself and winked at Leah across the desk. Maybe things would be OK after all. Leah scowled back at him.

'I can't do it,' she said. 'It'll be terrible.'

'It'll be fine. Forget the station, forget Sol, just close your eyes and be out in the street like you always are. Forget the studio boss.'

'He's the studio boss?' She looked terrified.

'One of them. Don't worry. Do some Tracey, and Joni, and Alanis, and Sheryl, oh yeah and Dido.'

'That's more than three.'

'So? If I'm gonna lose my job over this, I wanna go out in style.'

'You're gonna lose your job?' She looked terrified again.

He grinned and shrugged. 'Maybe,' he said.

Sol came back with water for Leah and a coffee for the studio boss. The exec positioned himself on a desktop and waited. Sol came in and sat next to Jake. Mosher indicated the countdown and they were on air. Jake opened his mouth to speak and Mosher bit into a pork pie the size of Paris.

The studio fell silent.

Jake stared at the mic and did what he always did: he saw one face, one listener, one guy sitting there over a pint, hanging on his every word.

Looking after number one 181

(When he once told Leah that you had to broadcast as if just one person were listening she said, 'Yeah – and in your case it's true.' When he told Rach the same thing, she replied, 'How can you be sure anyone's out there?')

The silence in the studio went on. Jake's radio life flashed in front of him. He'd been a chart keeper since the age of twelve. Small frayed exercise books filled with spidery lists of misspelled bands and half-remembered song titles. Information gleaned from huddling over his old wireless radio, bequeathed from an uncle. He'd lapped it up, and one listen of the weekly run-down so burned itself into his psyche that he could spend the rest of the week reciting the movers and shakers in the top twenty, the new entries and the highest climbers. He rarely found anyone interested but it didn't deter him. Little did he know that his love of the three-minute pop song and all the music trivia that went with it would one day secure him a spot in radio history. No one loved the music like Jake. No one did so much to evangelise the listener to his way of thinking. It was one thing to foam at the mouth about the commercial dross in the chart: it was quite another to be honest enough to admit that the only reason it was in the chart was because a heck of a lot of people actually liked it.

'Jake!'

It was Sol, nudging him in the ribs and indicating the mic with a tilt of his head.

Mosher was outside the glass, frowning, with bits of pork pie stuck to his thick lips. Beyond him, over his shoulder, the studio boss was staring incredulous and wide eyed. Across the studio, Leah was poised with her hand over her six string. Time stood still.

'Don't you think Bruce Springsteen should do a Christmas album?' Jake's voice suddenly kicked in, though it sounded six months out of date, like he'd switched on halfway through a tape from another show on another station.

'I mean his rendition of "Santa Claus is coming to town" has to be the best Christmas song in the history of the world, right? So why not a full festive album from his Bossness? "Frosty the snowman", "I saw Mommy kissing Santa Claus", "Wombling Merry Christmas", "Twinkle twinkle little star", "Grandma (we love you)" . . . What say you, average punters? I'd love to hear tonight. Perhaps you got some suggestions for covers Brucie could throw in, let's put the full might of our listening power into this one and get the best darn Christmas album in the world ever! Here's Apache Frost and after that Stevie B and the Shifty 6.'

Jake sat back in his seat and looked exhausted. 'Sorry,' he muttered, 'blanked out there for a minute.'

'Well, could you not do it when I'm about to sing live on radio for the first time, please?'

Leah's voice was hard now, the power had come back into it. Jake smiled.

'Sounds like you're good to go,' he said.

'Good? I'm gagging! Now let's get it on, Jimmy Saville!'

She sang like an angel. Pulled out all the stops and poured her heart into every word. Sol grinned his way through her set like a Cheshire cat on speed. She went from 'Thank you' to 'Sorry' without a stutter or a wrong note, and finished up with a perfect 'Big yellow taxi'.

Sol was up and signing a contract before she'd finished strumming.

'That was Leah Paddan, brightest new star in the galaxy. Watch out for her forthcoming single. Here's Tiger Trees and a great golden oldie, "Mudface".'

Looking after number one

When Jake glanced through the studio glass, the exec was grinning to himself and studying the relief on Leah's face. Sol magicked a bottle of champagne from nowhere and the others spent the next ninety minutes celebrating, while Jake took calls about this raging new talent, radio's next big thing; amidst of course, a million calls for Brucie to sing "Away in a manger" on his forthcoming Christmas album.

After the show, he and Sol sat in The Ladder and nursed pints.

'Been a long time, Sol, thanks for coming. Leah was well made up.'

'It was worth it: you weren't wrong. She's a star. My old man'll love her. She just needs a few great songs and she'll be the next Katie Melua.'

'You could write a few for her,' Jake said hopefully but Sol looked unsure.

'Maybe,' he said. 'She's needs a new name too. Leah . . . East. Yeah, that's got a good ring to it. Names are important, you know. By the way – what happened back there? At the start of the show, you looked like a total amateur for a while.'

'I felt like a total amateur. I dunno. Things are falling apart a bit at the moment. I don't want to talk about it right now. Maybe later.'

'OK, then I have a favour to ask, I need your help, mate. I'm trying to track down a missing girl. Abby Mann. You don't know her, do you?'

'Should I?'

Sol shook his head.

'Just a long shot.'

'You got any leads?'

'Well, her brother lives over in Peniel Green. Works in a pub there. I met him once and I reckon he knows something: maybe she told him she was going to disappear for a while. She could even be staying with him.'

'So what d'you want me to do?'

'Come with me. He's a big guy, unstable maybe. I'd feel happier questioning him with someone else there.'

'Does he know you're coming?'

Sol shook his head. 'No, but the landlady of the pub does, I told her I'd look in on her, but now that I think about it I reckon we go straight to his place. Surprise him.'

'Fine, we'll go tomorrow morning. I need a suitable distraction right now. Bit of derring-do never did any harm.'

They ordered a couple more pints and felt themselves slipping into a dark beery haze.

'D'you ever think much about school?' Sol said, and Jake laughed.

'I hated school,' he said. 'Esau was better than me at all the things that mattered. Sport, girls, mates, parties. The only things I could do were maths and music.'

'I have to confess, Jake – I don't remember you at all.'

Jake nodded. 'I thought as much,' he said.

Bitesize anecdotes

Later they went back to the chapel and sat in the graveyard, cupping whisky in their hands, their backsides warming the age-old inscriptions on a couple of tombstones.

'This girl, Abby,' Jake said, 'd'you think she's all right?'

Sol shivered. 'I've no idea. I hope she's done the sensible thing and run off to find a new life somewhere. No one's heard of her lately. She's vanished off the planet. Couldn't blame her for jacking in her parents: her family home is like a morgue.'

'Are you and she . . . you know?'

Sol laughed. 'If only, mate, if only. Too good for the likes of me.'

It was Jake's turn to laugh. 'When was any woman too good for the likes of you?'

Sol shrugged. 'Let's just say she was . . . out of reach.' He shook his head and added, 'Sadly.' He sighed, shifted his backside and lay back against the turf. Above the trees midnight black clouds drifted by like random days of his life.

'What about you and Leah?' he asked. 'Are you and she . . . you know?' and he added a melodramatic wink.

'Oh yes,' said Jake, and he shook his head and added, 'sadly.'

'Really? She's gorgeous. Amazing voice.'

Jake winced. 'She has a sister,' was all he said.

Somewhere an owl hooted and a fox cried. They listened and realised the place was alive with an audience. Sol traced the name on a nearby headstone with the toe of his designer shoe.

'D'you believe in God, Sol?' Jake asked.

'Yeah, I think I'm starting to – I had a kind of epiphany on the way over here.'

Jake laughed, and the laughter had an edge. 'I had one of those once. Saw the door of heaven sagging open and these dudes going up and down a ladder. Right in that spot where you're lying actually. Doubt if I'll get a second chance though.'

'My old man swears by all that. Music is the voice of God, he says.'

'My old man's the same. I just don't know though. It's like it was easier for them somehow – they believed and saw it all work. What was it I read recently, a quote from some psalm?' Jake took another swig of whisky, tiny brown droplets glistened on his top lip for a second, then he smeared them away and said, '"*Our ancestors trusted in you, and you rescued them. You heard their cries for help and saved them. They put their trust in you and were never disappointed.*" It was like that. They didn't question, didn't push the boundaries and it worked. I don't know that I can see it like that. Sol, you asked me about that blackout on the radio earlier. Feels like everything's coming at me. I keep having these dreams – nightmares . . .'

So he told Sol the story – every last detail.

At the end Sol sat up, poured them both more whisky and grinned. 'You know, I read about you recently,' he said.

'What?'

'Someone gave me this little black book . . .'

'Oh, not you an' all – why is everyone reading about me all of a sudden . . . ? It isn't me anyway. That's some other guy.'

'You know the outcome of the story?' Sol butted in. 'He goes back.'

'Yeah, and his brother kills him.'

'No, he faces up to reality – it does nearly finish him off – he ends up wrestling with an angel by a camp fire. They wrestle all night. It leaves him wasted – but changed.'

'I know that one, I read it,' said Jake, 'but it's not me in there, it's some other guy, some other ancient dude.'

'Yes, but the story goes on, doesn't it? I mean you don't need a little black book to find it. It's everywhere: in the papers, magazines, movies . . . age-old tale, mate. There's nothing original about you. People live that life all the time, every day. I heard this story on the radio once, about this anonymous girl who wrote in 'cause she was estranged from her mother. By the time the DJ had finished telling the story the phone lines were jammed with mothers calling in to ask – is it my daughter? No kidding. The country's full of warring families. You're just another battle statistic.'

Jake sat in bewildered silence and stared at Mo Mountain's grave.

'So what do I do?'

'You really want to know?'

'No . . . yes . . . I gotta stop these dreams.'

'Then you got to go home. Do the repentant prodigal thing and head back. Lick your wounds and wash off the pig shite.'

'Sounds great. Anyway – don't come the prodigal thing – I read that story too – that dude's motives are well mixed man, he goes back with a set speech, gets it all lined up so he can impress the old man.'

'So what's your point? You mean you don't have mixed motives? Come on, enough of this Oprah stuff, let's talk about girls and get drunk.'

Jake poured more whisky, staggered to Mo's grave and plonked himself on it.

'Wait, wait, wait. I got a story for you, Mr Sun-shines-out-of-your-backend-wiseman. I knew a guy once, happily married but couldn't stop himself from falling for other woman. One after the other. Bang, bang, bang. Suddenly, unexpectedly, his wife left him. Woke up and found himself alone. Immediately there's a queue of women at his door, all of them claiming the right to be the next wife. He could have his pick. And they were beautiful. But he didn't want any of them: took one look and ran a mile.'

'What's your point?'

'I dunno. It's just a story. I guess sometimes we only want what we haven't got 'cause we can't have it. When we can have it, we don't want it.'

'Yeah, and here's a bit more wisdom for you. People never learn anything from bitesize anecdotes you tell in a pub – or a graveyard – about alleged mates and their many women. You learn by experience. For better or worse. Monologues are for stand-up comedians. Great at the time but you can never remember them afterwards.'

They stood and clinked glasses and stared at the roaming mist, as it closed in on them like God's hand taking hold of their souls.

PART FOUR

The chase sequence

Cain stirred and sat up. His head felt as if it were full of damp cotton wool. Downstairs someone was putting up shelves, the hammering went on and on and on. No, not shelves, it was the door. Someone was hammering on the door. He hauled himself from his bed, pulled on a long, slowly unravelling jumper, and slunk downstairs. The hammering got louder, he walked to the door, freed the locks and swung it back.

'Yes?'

Two strangers with weird hair stood on the doorstep. One of them had blond spikes with fiery red tips: the tips were so red it looked as if his head was on fire. The other one looked vaguely familiar, but his hair didn't, it just looked stupid, like a bad throwback to the New Romantics of the eighties. The familiar one opened his mouth and spoke.

'You don't know us,' he said, 'but we think you've got a DVD of *Brief Encounter*. Deluxe edition?'

Cain ran. I mean, really ran. Pushed the stranger aside and belted down the path into the road. A passing car swerved, screeched and blared at him, the wing buffering against his hip, but Cain dodged in time to avoid any major injury. The driver stopped and leapt out, swearing as he came, but Cain didn't stop or look back. He legged it to the pub across the road and scrambled up and over the hedge. One of the Alsatians came at him, snapping and snarling but Cain slammed his fist inside its jaws and booted it away. The dog whimpered and retreated, leaving the way clear for Cain to slip down the side of the pub, hurdle the pile of empty barrels and make straight for the stile onto the public footpath beyond. Once there, he broke off the path and ducked through a gap in the hedge into the next field. Then he just ran, on and on and on until he reached the woods beyond. When he stopped to look back, he was under a huge oak tree and the blood was thundering in his ears. In the distance, the guy with the weird hair was just breaking through the hedge, stomping up and down, looking wildly around, but he had not seen Cain: he had no idea where the fugitive was. Cain slumped down, leaning against the tree and panting hard. He stayed there for a long time. All day, in fact. Fear glued him to the spot. He didn't eat, didn't move.

He just sat in the dust, waiting for the light to die and the hunters to leave him alone. Eventually the sky darkened. He rose stiffly and crept back towards the pub and the road. There in the yellow street-lit darkness he spied on his own home. Damn.

The guy with the crimson and blonde hair had gone: he was nowhere to be seen but the stranger with the uneven cut was still there, squatting by the door. It was past midnight and he was still sitting on the step. Why wouldn't he go? Cain crouched in the shadows and willed the guy to give up. But no response; no way was that stranger packing up for the night. That meant Cain couldn't get to his Skoda, he was stuck on foot. That's when he decided to break into the pub. There was bound to be a latch loose somewhere on the shambolic Memphis. There had to be. Terrified the dogs might still

The chase sequence

be on the prowl, he crept down the alley beside the pub and squinted at the windows. All shut and locked. Tamar was thorough. He went round the back and pressed his face to the kitchen window. The glass was cold and greasy against his skin. There inside, between him and the rest of the pub were Ammo and Jude, for now soundly asleep and still slavering as they dreamt.

That would have been fine except for one tiny little fact. The kitchen window was latched half open. It was the only one that gave access. A helluva lot of courage and very little effort would see him inside.

He slipped his hand up and in, between the window and the frame and strained to loose the catch. Jude shifted and licked his lips. Ammo's ears flickered and wilted. Cain soldiered on. His fingers seemed huge and unwieldy, the catch too fine and tiny. But he flapped his hand repeatedly and suddenly he made contact: the catch flew up and he was in. He crouched on the draining board, hunched like a human vulture, then lowered himself to the floor and made it out of the kitchen and up the stairs.

He stood in her room and watched her sleep. Tamar was very different when she wasn't awake. The cool exterior slipped away from her. Her face was relaxed, her forehead smooth, all the front was gone. Her make-up lay in tubs and sticks beside the bed. Here was the real woman, the one with peace on her face instead of powder. She was beautiful when she was awake, swanning about like Cleopatra, but here, now, here was her real beauty. And it was nothing to do with the junk she normally put out to impress. This was innocence and honesty: a woman at peace with the world because she had no idea the world was watching. He sat and studied her for a long time. He studied the curve of her flesh and bones, her figure outlined through the thin sheet. He studied that clean open face and those pale lips, stripped of their gloss. She was everything he wanted and he couldn't tear his eyes away. Why was life so contradictory? Why was she so brittle in daylight and so warm in the night? It didn't take much to ignite someone like Cain and, boy, he was alight now. He continued to stare at her. Basking in the knowledge no one had the first idea where he was. Not even her. He stepped to the foot of her bed and gently touched her foot through the sheet. She snorted and stirred and her face hardened in her sleep. He pulled back. He needed money. That's what he needed. The other bits of her would only get him in trouble. He went looking. There was a huge dressing table on the far side of her bed.

He eased the top drawer open and stared. It was full of photos of men. He looked across at her. What was that about? Former boyfriends? Or something else? Everyone had their darkness. If anyone knew about that, he did. He closed the drawer and opened the next one down. Underwear. The full spectrum – from substantial to insignificant. He ran his hand over it, then stopped himself. Money. Concentrate. Nothing else mattered. Anything else was dangerous. He turned to glance at her again and his eyes fell on a fat leather bag lying beside the bed. He practically fell on it and wrenched the zip open. Inside was her purse, a serious black leather pouch with a bunch of twenties oozing from it. He felt the betrayal as he tore the notes out but it was his only chance now. As he knelt in the semi-darkness he caught his reflection in her bedside mirror. What had happened to him? He used to be so principled. Had the passing of time eroded his sanity? He barely recognised the villain crouching here with stolen money in his fist. The eyes leering back at him were bleak and hollow; two empty caverns punched in a face of dead rock.

He stood up and stared at her one last time. One long last time. He'd discovered a whole lot about her in the last three minutes. She stirred and rolled over and turned towards him, but her eyes were closed and her face was calm. Her arm lay across the sheet, the hand reaching for him. It was a tempting offer. But he knew it was all in his head. In reality Tamar could give him nothing. He tore himself away. On the way down the stairs he looked out the window. The stranger was still lurking by his door. Renegade's Rest would get no peace tonight. There was a sudden snarl and Cain leapt back up two steps. One of the dogs was at the bottom of the stairs: eyes raging like molten lava, teeth bare and dripping thick sticky spit. Which dog was it? Ammo or Jude? He hoped like hell it was Jude. He took a step forward, the dog tensed his legs and pushed his face forward. The snarling grew louder. Cain braced himself. He took another step. The dog let out a bark; just what he didn't need. Tamar would come running and the other dog too. Between them they'd rip him to shreds. He couldn't stand it: he hurled himself down the stairs and flattened the dog with his body. The Alsatian yelped and rolled free. Cain braced himself for teeth in the back of his neck or ripping into his calves where his jeans had rucked up. Nothing. He looked up. The dog was gone. It had been Jude, and the memory of the kick he had given the dog in the yard earlier had saved him.

Cain sighed and collapsed on the bottom step of the stairs.

'That was lucky . . .'

But it wasn't. He hadn't kicked the other beast and, woken by the noise, Ammo appeared in the doorway. Cain took one look and turned and bounded back upstairs. He crashed into Tamar's bedroom and the noise woke her like a bucket of ice water. She shot up and gaped at him. She blinked profusely and said nothing. The thin sheet fell away and they both glanced down at her body.

'What are you doing here?' she whispered as she pulled the sheet back up.

'I . . .' What was the use? He had no cover story.

'Ammo! Stay!'

The dog was hovering, desperate for the kill.

'Well?' she said.

'It's . . . complicated.'

She picked up her mobile and pressed a few buttons. 'I could call the police, you know,' she said.

He nodded, but somehow he knew her heart wasn't in it.

'You'd better get out of here. Did you break anything?'

He shook his head. 'A loose latch downstairs helped me.'

'I don't understand you, one minute you're all subservient and "Yes, ma'am, No, ma'am", the next you're creeping about in my house after dark.'

'We all have our . . . unexpected sides,' he muttered. His eyes fell on the bag beside the bed.

'Tell me what's going on in that head of yours, Cain,' she said.

If he'd have been at work, he might have done. If it had been daylight, things would have been different. But it was the dead of night outside and he was in a bad way.

They eyeballed each other. Her face softened unexpectedly. 'Stay with me,' she said suddenly.

'What?'

'You want to, don't you? I'm not that repellent, am I?'

He didn't know what to say. Of course he wanted to stay. It was the one thing in the world he wanted, but there had to be a price tag. A woman like Tamar didn't just offer this.

She let the sheet fall again but he didn't look this time.

'I . . . I'm in trouble . . .' he muttered.

'So am I. Don't go.'

'What?'

She leant across the bed and grabbed his hand. He felt himself falling toward her.

'Men mess you up,' she said. 'But . . .' she gave him a coy smile, 'for some reason I'm starting to trust you.'

'You don't know me.'

'I think I know more than you think I know.'

'I don't understand that.'

She laughed and her face lit up. He'd never seen her happy before. But it was no use: he couldn't stay. He knew he couldn't stay. He was sitting on the edge of the bed now. She was stroking his leg.

'Tamar, this isn't gonna happen.'

She ignored him. 'Men screw you up, you know,' she said.

He said nothing.

'What's this? The black mark still there then.'

She ran a hand over the back of his fist. The black mark had morphed into something resembling a dark mask etched on the skin.

'Man, that's ugly,' she said, and she laughed. 'Looks scary.'

'Then don't touch it,' he said.

'Oops! Too late,' she said and she traced the shape with her finger.

'I was married, you know,' she said. 'Twice. They both died.'

'You're kidding.'

Her face hardened. 'Do I look like I'm kidding? I mean – how unlucky can you get? One in a train wreck, one up a mountain. Sounds like the start of a joke, doesn't it?' She ran her hand over his. 'Men leave you. Or they abuse you.'

She pinched the skin on the back of his hand. Hard. Then she looked away.

'Death isn't abuse,' Cain said.

'I'm not talking about my husband. I'm talking about . . . his father.'

She looked back and pulled him down. He was gonna give in, he could feel it.

'I know a dozen customers who'd kill to be where you are now,' she said.

'I believe it. If I wasn't in a tight corner right now . . .'

'What kind of corner?'

He shook his head.

'What kind of corner?'

'Too complicated.'

'Everything's complicated.'

He started to reach for her shoulder, in his head he already had his hands on her. It was going to happen. It was too late. His brain had just left the building and his groin was in charge now. There was nothing he could do.

'What's that in your hand?'

She was staring at the fistful of notes.

'What?'

'Is that my money? It is, isn't it? You were gonna run with my money?'

'I told you, it's complicated.'

She balled her fist and smacked him across the chin, then she caught him a second time on the other side with the flat of her hand. The sound of the slap was loud enough to blank out the torrent of her swearing.

She tore the notes from his hand and shoved him hard off the bed. 'Get out!' she yelled. 'Get out!'

The chase sequence

It was too loud: weird guy across the road was bound to have heard it. Cain glanced towards the gap in her curtains, the window was open a little. The dogs started barking, it was turning into a right old nightmare.

'GET OUT!'

She really yelled it this time and out in the street there was the sound of approaching feet thudding on the tarmac.

She screamed at him again and he saw his chance, the notes flapping in her hand. He leapt, grabbed them back and tore out of the room. Ammo was coming at him but he was in full flow now, one boot and the dog fell sprawling. He jumped down the stairs four at a time, yanked open the locks on the pub door and threw himself into the night.

Behind him running steps rattled down the side of the building, so for the second time that day he crossed the yard and vaulted the style into the field and off towards the trees. Only this time he'd been seen. Weird guy was on his tail. There'd be no hiding in the woods this time. He turned and fled across the grass. He ran so hard and so long that spit gummed up his mouth like glue. His lungs contorted and screamed at him to stop. But he went on. Run, mate, run, and don't stop till you find another Renegade's Rest in another Peniel Green somewhere.

Sol sat on the step and sighed. He'd been there all day, with just a break for lunch at The Memphis. He pulled the hip flask from his pocket. It felt sleek and smooth in his hands, a perfect fit when he weighed it in his palm. He loosed the silver cap and let it fall and hang down on the little leather strand. His grandfather had given it to him. Jesse. A big guy with a huge family and a passion for his God the size of Wembley Stadium. Jesse had been the man all right. Uncomplicated, kind, dedicated. A million miles from his grandson. But then his grandson inhabited a different world. You could survive as Jesse in Jesse's world: in Sol's world you had to be something else.

Sol knocked back the flask and felt the Jack Daniels burn his lips. So much whisky in so little time. But he didn't care. He needed the Dutch courage right now.

Suddenly there was a yell from the house across the road. He pocketed the drink and stood up. There it was again. Another yell. No, it wasn't the house. It was the pub. He started running, his feet pounding the road as he fled towards the noise. Another yell, and dogs barking. He made the hedge, looked for a way over and found a gate. He vaulted it and heard the sound of a door opening. A dimly lit path ran down the left side of the pub so he took it. There in the distance was Cain, his unmistakable Mohawk silhouetted against the night sky. Sol gave chase across the yard and followed him over the stile to the path and field beyond. Sol's ankle twisted and gave as he landed on the other side and he was forced to stop for a moment to get his breath. How did he get here? Twisted ankle in a strange field in the middle of nowhere at midnight. All for a stupid DVD.

Back at Renegade's Rest, Jake circled the cottage. Sol had disappeared, run off while he was searching round the back. Jake checked the place now for an easy way in. There didn't appear to be one. The windows were shut and there was only the one entrance. For a while he squatted on the doorstep, getting colder, but sure that Sol would return before too long. As the night closed its fingers around him, his senses heightened and tuned to the sounds nearby. He was not alone. The hedges around the house rustled frequently, creatures crept by in the moonlight and at one point he was sure he clocked a rat. The place was alive and it made him nervous; little eyes flickering in the dark, predatory noises coming at him through the blackness. His mind drifted back to Bethel and his familiar graveyard. Odd, he felt more at ease among the dead than the living.

A footstep. He had placed his head against the door frame and was just drifting off when he heard it. He snapped his head round. Was someone there in the dark? Was it the guy with the Mohawk back to kill him? He leapt up and backed away, listening all the time. His heel connected with something on the ground, a broken barrel buried in the grass. He twisted to pull free but his foot was wedged between the wood and the turf. He yanked hard, slipped and fell back. His hand landed on something warm, something moving. Fur struggled and wrestled free beneath his fingers. He yelped and scrambled up. That was it: he'd had enough of Renegade's Rest. He went back out to the road and sat on the grassy bank there. He knew he was in for a sleepless night. He'd never be able to switch off now. He stared at The Memphis and willed the day to arrive. He was still doing this when he drifted off, slipped down the bank and ended up in a ditch beside the road.

The table

Cain wandered into the park and collapsed on a bench. Then he heard the noise. The sound of sucking and belching and careless chewing. He looked up and saw them. It was three in the morning and someone was having a tea party in the park.

There was a massive table with a dozen tramps round it, shoving food down their throats. He looked around for the cameras – it had to be some kind of TV stunt.

Nope.

Nothing. Just the night and twelve tramps round a table. Then a dark figure stepped up.

'Don't panic,' he said, 'it's just, er . . . an experiment.'

Cain looked at the roughly hewn faces, the spiky beards, the red noses and black eyes, the broken teeth and spattered jackets.

The stranger held out his hand. Why was he so friendly? People weren't usually so friendly.

'I'm doing an experiment. A kind of last supper for the planet. See that table: so far it's been to Tibet, Brazil and Siberia. Straight up. Not kidding. Flown it all over the world. This is the England bit.'

'The England bit of what?'

'The trip. Taking bread and wine to the people. It was theirs all the time but it got taken from them. Took it to a football club last night, an art gallery the night before. Want something to eat?'

The table

'You're nuts.'

'Maybe – but these guys don't care. You look as if you've been through the mill a bit.'

'Then I'm in good company,' Cain said and he nodded towards the guests round the table.

The man laughed. 'Come join us,' he said. 'No one'll mind. The body and blood come to you whoever you are, but it's not easy to accept it. These guys love it, they have nothing to lose. You should have seen 'em at the art gallery – walking out in droves they were.'

'I don't get it,' Cain said. Then he spotted the dog collar. 'You're a minister of the church?'

He was suspicious now.

'Maybe, but all I wanna do is offer something. Look, would you read this for me, I've been doing this for six months now, all over the planet, and I'm a little . . . familiar with it.'

He handed Cain a book with a steel cover and steered him to the table.

As he got closer Cain caught the smell of sweat, urine, wine and fresh bread. It was a heady mixture. The guy nodded and grinned again. He was tall and thin, but with a protruding beer gut, like a pregnant beanpole. He gestured to Cain, encouraging him to read.

'"On the night he was betrayed he took some bread, tore it into bits and handed it round. This is my body, he said, I'm giving my life for you, it'll be ripped and devoured like this bread."'

As Cain read, the man of God took a fresh loaf and tore it up, nudged a few of the tramps and passed it round. They took little notice and just shoved it in along with the meat and vegetables they were already chewing.

'Do I have to do this? Only I'm in a hurry and no one's listening . . .'

The pregnant beanpole had a bottle of Pinot Noir in his hand. 'Keep going,' he muttered. 'You're doing great . . .'

Cain studied the guy's face. He had bulky curly hair, a smattering of scars and a broken nose. He clearly hadn't been a vicar all his working life. He uncorked the bottle and waved it at Cain. 'I know what you're thinking. Stupid, right?'

Cain shrugged and looked at the men shoving food in like they were shovelling cement into a mixer. He shook his head and read on. '"Then he took some wine, poured it out and handed it round. This is like my blood, he said, spilled for you. Drink it and think about my sacrifice. Corrupt leaders are only in it for themselves, the good leader gives himself for the people."'

As the guy poured generous rations into nearby glasses, some of the wine missed and red spurts exploded across the table like fatal bullet wounds.

'Can I go now?' Cain said.

He nodded. 'Thank you,' he said. 'Oh, one more thing.' And he handed Cain a cup of wine and a hunk of bread.

'Take these. You never know when you'll next need it.'

Cain downed the cup slowly and steadily, with unusual reverence, as if he was drinking his first and last communion.

'Oi!' A yell from the gate. It was one of those guys again, the one with the uneven hair. They just wouldn't give up. Neither would Cain. He took off.

He hurled himself across the field and lurched his way towards the hedge on the far side. He heard the thunder of his own breathing and the thud of feet behind him but he didn't look back. He ran on and found himself scrambling up and over the hedge. Thorns and jagged twigs dug into his skin and tore strips from his clothes. He fought them off and flipped himself over onto the other side. He was on a road heading away from civilization. Perfect. He hurled down it, running for a long time until he spotted a gate to his left. He clambered over and found himself in another field, full of corn, a solid wall of yellow. He threw himself into it and scrambled on his hands and knees, and immediately he was lost. It would either deliver or destroy him. He couldn't see the way out, but then he couldn't see anything. So he stopped scrambling and curled up in the dark.

In his head he was back in his cupboard. Back in the big old wardrobe at home, safe in the darkness and in the sweet knowledge that he was secure. He always went into the wardrobe in the hope that the back would be missing and replaced by snow and children in fur coats with posh accents. But it was never the case. It was disappointing, then reassuring. And he was happy to settle for second best. Happy to hide from the world, the world of his smarter sister and his angry father. His dad was always angry, like something had hacked him off early in life and he was still looking for someone to blame.

Someone was coming. Someone was barging their way through the long grain, gasping and trampling and sniffing him out. So he stopped scrambling and lay there in the dark, imagined himself to be invisible and suddenly felt desperately tired. The footsteps came closer, then receded, then came back. He pushed himself into the dirt, willing the ground to open up. A foot landed right by his left eye. The toe twisted and thudded by his left cheek. Cain lay still, shut his eyes tight and waited. Another step, then another. When he opened his eyes, the foot was gone.

Running and hiding

He woke up with a start. The dawn was breaking like a bad rash across the sky.

Somewhere in the distance someone was playing 'Everybody's got something to hide except me and my monkey' by the Beatles. Two great eyes surrounded by hair peered down at him. His first thought was of Ammo. The evil wolverine was back to finish him off. But the nose was black and striped and was too much like a fat hosepipe. Something in Cain's head put two and two together and he remembered that badgers can be dangerous. He leapt up, screamed and kicked dirt in its face. The badger moved back, looking only a little startled, then coughed, turned and waddled away. It was an underwhelming response but at least it got rid of the creature.

The music changed to 'Hitsville UK' by the Clash. He stood up and looked around. There were yellow stalks everywhere and no paths. He spun in a 360-degree circle and every direction looked the same. Pick a stalk and push on through, it was all he could do. He started walking. The corn pulled at his clothes and scratched his skin, but he went on. Eventually, having cut an untidy swathe through the field, he blundered out and found himself beside a hedge. The music changed to 'One more night' by Yellow Dog. It was coming from a nearby tractor: a huge green dinosaur with bug-eyed lamps on the front. In the cab a small farmer with a huge cap was chewing on a sandwich.

'You're up early,' the farmer yelled, pushing open the cab door. 'You haven't damaged that corn have you? Not crop circles, is it?'

He laughed at his own joke, his red face turning redder. Cain went closer. 'What time is it?'

'Five thirty. Where you off to at this time?'

'No idea,' Cain muttered and he pushed past the tractor and made for the gate.

He thought about heading back but he knew it wasn't worth it now. Maybe in a few days but he needed to lie low for a while. No more Renegade's Rest, no more Tamar and The Memphis. Just running again. Running and hiding. Seemed like it would never end.

The coffee shop

Jake sat up in the ditch, his phone shrieking in his fingers. The signal was desperately weak and he could barely make out Sol's voice.

'Sol, where are you? Where? What happened? What?' He listened and scowled. 'Back where? You're kidding! That's miles. I said, that's miles. I'll jump in the car. Stay in the High Street, I'll see you outside Boots. Boots! Boots! Don't go anywhere. Stay put. Stay pu . . . oh great.'

The connection died. He shut the phone and ran to the car. Mohawk man was giving them the right runaround.

Cain found himself a table in the corner and sat there twisting the menu in his hands. It had a perfectly round coffee stain on the cover. He flipped it open and stared at lines of writing which meant little. Back and forth he let his eyes flit between his fingers. One or two flecks of red were still stuck under his fingernails. He frowned, pressed the corner of the menu under his left thumbnail and eased it along the compressed flesh. A tiny shard of dried blood curled along and jumped out onto the table.

'What can I get you?'

She looked like his sister, though of course she couldn't be. This demure waitress with the willing smile and the short blonde hair.

'Americano, please.'

'Anything to eat?'

He ordered bacon and waffles with extra syrup. She went and he leant forward again and studied the street through the window. The chase had robbed him of much appetite, but he had to keep his energy up. Sugary junk might just do it. As he sat and waited his mind jumped backwards, meandering through his last days like a recap. *Previously in Cain's life* . . . And he saw again his sister's book, that precious black leather book. And he saw himself riffling through it, experiencing something like an electric shock as he came across the strange account of one brother killing another, one brother jealous of his sibling, one brother who felt unaccepted and unacceptable, who ended up running, cursed, forever condemned to a life of ducking and diving. It was like looking in a mirror. In his mind, he flicked backwards in the book and, sure enough, there was his father. Digging away in a garden, living a good and peaceful life, a life before kids and families and complications. He shook his head and snapped out of the memory.

Nearby a lone copy of *The Independent* sprawled across a table top. He scooped it up and flicked pages. A decade after the event a doctor, first on the scene when Diana died, was reported as claiming that he thought she might live. That story was gonna run and run. A first edition of *Wuthering Heights* had sold for £114,000. Cain could do with that kind of money right now. In the background Joe Jackson sang about girls and how it was different for them. Cain's life was passing in front of his eyes. He was trying to think about coffee and news and pop music, but there were other things crowding it out. His life had become too dark, too imposing: he couldn't hide from his history. In the paper a young girl had been found dead in the street. That was too close to home. A celebrity was in court over some restraining order, and British people couldn't do geography. Apparently a third of the population thought Everest was in Europe. His bacon and waffles arrived: it smelt great but suddenly he wasn't hungry, the dead girl in the paper had stolen his appetite. A stolen dog had been returned for £750 ransom. The police weren't happy about the capitulation by the owners. Dog owners of the world were all in peril now.

He bit into some bacon and turned a page. The rich and famous stared back at him, all of them in custody: the likes of Bill Gates, Steve McQueen and Zsa Zsa Gabor had all spent time inside. The great and the good had become the bad and the ugly. Some were no surprise: Sid Vicious, Fidel Castro. I mean, what else did you expect? But Frank Sinatra? Admittedly it was only for carrying on with a married woman (back in 1938 that was practically a hanging offence) but still – old blue eyes on skid row? Raging Doors' front man, Jim Morrison, apparently got his collar felt for (shock horror) attacking a policemen's helmet. Life was tough back in the swinging sixties.

Cain had read enough, the news was getting as bonkers as his life. He got up, left his food and slipped out without paying. The waitress returned to find it really wasn't her day.

'Seen a tall guy – real beanpole? Mohican hair. Bit messed up, looked like he was on the run?'

The waitress eyed the two guys carefully. This was definitely a day for memorable hair.

'Why?' she said.

'Why not? Have you seen him? Did he come in? Someone down the road said . . .'

The coffee shop

She nodded. 'But you're not going to beat him up, are you?'

'No!' said the one with the Human League cut. 'Believe it or not, we want to ask him about a DVD.'

'Which one?'

'What does it matter which one?'

'Just wondered.'

'Well, it's not *Notting Hill*, all right?'

'Ha ha. Not every woman likes Hugh Grant you know. Matt Damon maybe . . .'

'Look, we're in a hurry, right . . .' The one with red and blonde spikes said, starting to leave.

'Have you seen *Amélie*?' she asked.

The New Romantic's face lit up. 'Yeah, brilliant. And the next one, *A Very Long Engagement* – though the title gives it away a bit.'

'I love Audrey Tautou,' she said. 'Though what she was doing in *The Da Vinci Code* I'll never know.'

'Excuse me, Mariella Frostrup,' said the blond one, 'Can we just go please? We're in a hurry.'

She shrugged. 'Just chatting,' she said. They went to the door and yanked it open.

'What was it then? The film I mean . . .' she asked as the bell rattled.

The Phil Oakey cut looked back. '*Brief Encounter*.'

'I worked in an underwear shop called that once,' was all she said and they ran.

The search

They chased up and down the high street, searching shops and cafés and doorways. But there was no sign of Cain. He'd really disappeared. They sagged in the doorway to Marks & Spencer and caught their breath. Jake felt as if he was going to cough up a lung. He'd not done this much physical exercise in a long time.

'I'm going home,' he said eventually, when he could talk again.

'What d'you mean?'

'I have to go back to settle things with my brother. I need to strike a deal with him. And I'm gonna have a kid. I have to see Esau and then I have to go home.'

'But what about all this? What about Abby?'

'Leave it to the cops. We don't have anything anyway. We've lost her brother.'

'Come on.' Sol grabbed Jake's shoulder. 'Let's talk about this over some good food. I'm starving.'

'OK, so you want to sort out your life, fine. But do one thing. Just one thing. Come back to Peniel Green with me. Come back and check over Cain's cottage. Then you can go off and do the prodigal son routine.'

'Why should I?'

'A favour for a favour. Remember?'

'That's not fair.'

The search

'Your girl, Leah, she wants a break, I have a shedload and I'm desperate to help her. She deserves it. You scratch my back and all that.'

Jake forked a load of prawns into his mouth. He washed them down with a mouthful of Guinness and grimaced before nodding. He had no choice; he understood the language of wheeler dealing. He'd grown up with it.

'But that's it. Just that one thing. We go back, we check the place and I leave.'

Sol nodded. 'Done and dusted,' he said.

Renegade's Rest stood in glorious sunlight as they strolled up. The Memphis was still shut and there was no sign of Tamar, but that was just as well. They didn't need witnesses to what they were going to do. Sol checked the road one last time, then they hopped over the wall and slipped around the back.

'We just need a cracked windowpane,' Sol muttered as they scrutinised the rear of the building. 'Just a tiny vulnerable spot.'

'There isn't one, mate, I checked last night,' moaned Jake.

'Absolutely,' Sol nodded and then he pointed. 'Right there.'

Sure enough, there was a small cracked windowpane.

'Why didn't I see that?' said Jake.

Sol elbowed the weak spot, and fumbled inside for the window latch.

Jake checked the road again, but no one had heard. Peniel Green was as quiet as death. He returned to Sol and they helped each other inside.

'Grief, it's gloomy in here. Like a dead man's Aladdin's cave or something.' Jake fingered some of the dusty ornaments over the fireplace but Sol was getting on with the job in hand.

'Come on,' he said. 'No time for playing Scooby Doo. You check upstairs, I'll search down here.'

'I'm not going up there alone.'

'Don't be a loser. Just get up and look.'

Jake took the stairs two at a time, the creaks and wheezes from the floor following him all the way up. He whistled an old punk tune as he thudded around from room to room, and eventually found himself in Cain's bedroom. He flopped on the bed and lay back.

What were they looking for anyway? There was nothing here to find. It was all useless – except for the fact that it would get Leah a recording contract. That made it worth something.

Jake glanced up at the ceiling. There was a tiny key hooked on one of the beams up there just below a tangled mesh of cobwebs.

Who would hook a key up high like that, and why? He'd have to check it. Jake stood up and reached for it. Someone had recently punched a hole in the tangled webs up there. That key had been removed and put back. This was looking interesting.

'Look!'

Jake thrust the cobwebbed metal into Sol's face. Sol backed off and scowled.

'So?'

'So it was hidden way up in the beams and someone's used it recently.'

Sol took the key, polished it on his jeans and studied it. 'It's for a grandfather clock.'

'What? How do you know that?'

'We had one like this. Drove me mad. Tick tick ticking all the time, chiming when you're trying to get down with the girls. Nightmare.'

'But we haven't heard any ticking since we've been in here. Or chiming.'

Sol grinned. 'You know what that means don't ya?'

Jake nodded: for once they were on the same wavelength. 'It's not working.'

'And the question is – why?'

'We have to find it first.'

Jake bounded back up the stairs, flinging open doors and cupboards in his haste. But there was nothing up there. Plenty of old gadgets and trinkets, but nothing anywhere near big enough for a grandfather clock.

Sol was waiting for him at the bottom of the stairs. He grimly shook his head and sighed.

'Shouldn't have had that second pint of Guinness,' Jake said. 'I'm down on stamina. Maybe it's not a grandfather clock, maybe it's just a music box or something. That could be hidden anywhere.'

'Maybe. Seen anything like that?'

'Plenty of little ghoulish trinkets around. But I haven't been looking properly.' He shivered. 'When does my contract run out?'

'You have to stay till we find something, mate. You promised. A favour for a favour.'

Jake frowned and strolled into the kitchen. 'I need some water,' he said, 'that'll clear my head . . . wait a minute.'

Sol followed him. Jake was staring out of the window. 'I bet you ain't been in there.'

He was pointing at the outhouse. Sol's face broke into a grin. 'Probably full of rats and cockroaches. But there'll still be room for a big old grandpappy clock.'

Jake stared at the rotten shell of a building. 'Off you go then,' he said.

Sol turned and pulled Jake with him. They tugged on the cottage front door. It opened easily.

'Oh, brilliant,' said Sol. 'We broke a window and the door was open all the time. Cain just ran, didn't he? He didn't have time to lock anything.'

Jake looked crestfallen. 'I don't believe it,' he said. 'I spent all last night in a ditch when I could have been snug in here.'

Sol glanced around and curled his lip. 'Snug ain't quite the word I'd use,' he said.

Jake shrugged and shook his head wearily. He was wasted, the last twelve hours had felt like a week. He shoved Sol. 'Let's get it done,' he said. 'You got the key?'

Sol waved it. They went.

The old building had once been whitewashed. Back in the days when Noah was Ronsealing the ark. The walls were now a filthy grey, with lashings of moss intermingled with streaks of crusted slurry.

There was no door, just an old farm gate upended and squeezed in the gap to keep animals out. Judging by the smell it didn't work. They worked the gate free and Sol tossed it to one side. The place was like a ransacked tomb: even in the sunlight it was bleak and dark inside. There were no windows.

'Used to be a coal house once upon a time,' Sol said, sweeping cobwebs from his face, 'what d'you reckon?'

'I reckon that's an old clock.'

A huge antique filled the far wall, the wood splintered and dented. It was a bigger timepiece than either of them had ever seen. The front was all cracks and gashes and the face had long since dropped off. It towered in the darkness, the size of a full-grown man, looking for all the world like an Egyptian burial case. And there, halfway down the front, over to the left-hand side, was

The search

a little keyhole. Just about the size of the one they were looking for.

'Go on then.' Jake nudged Sol, but Sol was reluctant to move.

'There'll be nothing in there,' Jake said. 'Probably a couple of porn mags and Yellowbeard's treasure map. Go on.'

Sol walked forward, his foot kicking against a can as he went. He clutched the key in his fist and his hand moved as if it was stuck in slow motion. Inch by inch he reached closer, but it was taking forever.

'Oh, give it here,' Jake's impatience kicked in and he grabbed the key and jammed it in the lock. He put it in so fast the key went in skewed and Jake ended up wrestling to yank it back out again. Sol piled in too and eventually the two of them pulled it free and Sol slipped it back inside with a little more grace. He sucked in air as he paused then turned the key. There was a tiny insignificant click, and the door fell open.

Neither of them expected what they found. The dead eyes of Abby, still open, still staring at the world, now looking straight at them. Her mouth hung down and lipstick was smeared across her bloodless, rotting right cheek. Her crumbling body was concertinaed into a space too small for it; blood had dried around her nose and eyes and green bruising rose in little swollen mounds on her neck, like volcanoes on a scale model. Her battered arms were pressed across her chest and clutched in her fingers were Celia Johnson and Trevor Howard – the deluxe version of *the best movie in the world*. That black and white cover mottled and spattered with Abby's lifeblood, the red patches colouring that famous *Brief Encounter* pose. Her favourite film sporting the marks of her death.

The battle

Sol turned away and threw up into the far corner. Jake just stared into those soulless eyes. One thought welled up like lava in his brain.

'You never told me we were looking for this. This is murder. I can't get mixed up in this.'

Sol staggered round and turned back towards the clock, wiping the back of his hand across his mouth as he came.

'I'm gonna be a dad,' Jake said, 'I can't get embroiled in this.'

'You're already embroiled in it, you doghead.'

Jake shook his head. He started to back out of the little building; he realised now the stench of decay had not been coming from a dead animal.

'Listen!' Sol gripped his shoulder. 'If you go, you're doing what you always do. Running. If you don't stay here and see this through, then nothing's changed. You won't stay with that kid of yours and you won't face up to your family. Don't you understand? This is the start of it. It begins here in this shitehole with a dead girl. Stop running.'

Jake frowned. 'What are you talking about?'

'I'm no idiot, Jake. I can read you like a book. You got the headlines all over your face, mate. Stop running. Do something good for once.'

'I do something good every night. I do my show and I make people feel better.'

The battle

'From a distance, mate. From your little empire behind that sound desk. Where no one can touch you or make you do something that's beyond your control. Well, you're out of your depth now, mate. It's sink or swim. Life is messy, it's sordid and you can't control it, you've gotta wrestle with it. Don't run just 'cause it feels out of control.'

Jake's face hardened and casually he reached down and picked up a split fence post. There were three nails in the top, all of them rusted.

'No one knows I've been here today, only you . . .'

'Oh yeah, that's great. Be another Cain. Kill your way out of trouble. That's perfect. Who will you murder next? Your brother?'

Jake swung the wood at Sol's head, but Sol ducked and smacked his shoulder into Jake's stomach. Then he ran him back until his body crashed into the clock. Jake felt Abby's cold fingers brushing against the back of his neck. He could smell the poison oozing from her dead flesh. It made him all the more scared and he lifted Sol up and flung him across the brickhouse. Then he ran for the door, but flailing fists smashed into his ankles and tripped him. He fell headlong and his face scraped against the wall as he went down. He tried to crawl from the wreckage but Sol grabbed him and hauled him to his feet.

'What's it to be?' Sol demanded.

'I can't stay here, you . . .'

Before he could finish Sol punched him across the jaw. Jake spun and fell onto his knees.

This was it. The thought struck him like a high-speed train. This was the dream. Only it wasn't Mosher, or Leah, or some tramp in a back alley. He was wrestling with a stranger in a dung-infested outhouse in the middle of nowhere. This wasn't supposed to be the way it happened. A boot thwacked into his back, knocking the air from his lungs.

'Fight, you coward, get up and fight. Stop running.'

Sol hauled him up, Jake gasping for air. Sol dragged him across the room and stood him up against the wall beside the old clock. Sol raised an arm and in his fist, jutting out like a jagged stalactite, was a rusty oil-stained chisel.

'Where the hell d'you get that?'

'Just reached out and there it was. Maybe an angel was waiting in the dark. Now, d'you still wanna run?'

'I can't stay here, I've gotta . . . Arggh!'

Jake let out a barbed string of ungodly language, peppering the air for a good few seconds.

It was a suitable description of the pain induced as Sol jammed the chisel into his thigh and twisted the blade back and forth in the wound as if he were winding the old grandfather clock.

'You asked for that,' he said coldly and stepped away.

But Jake wasn't done yet.

Fuelled by the pain, his anger gave him new strength and he lashed out and smacked Sol across the face. So hard that it spun him round twice and sent him the length of the room.

Then he stood panting and grimacing as he stared at the handle of the chisel, still protruding from his leg.

'Why d'you do that?' he screamed.

'To stop you running.'

'You barely know me.'

'I can't let you walk away. I can't be here alone with that body. We need each other to verify the story. And you need to do some growing up. If you're gonna be a dad, then in some bizarre, twisted way, all that starts here and now.'

The battle

Jake stood panting, the sweat glistening like dew on his face. Sol sat up and wiped blood and grime from his bottom lip.

'You know what your name means, Jake? *Grasper. Deceiver*. It says it in the black book. Did you read that bit? You wanna be that forever? Come on – be someone else, Jake. Get a new name. You're gonna be a dad, mate, this is a new start for you. A whole new country.'

Jake sneered. 'Grief, you're really some kind of philosopher, aren't you?'

'Nope, I'm just a talent scout, which means I can see potential when it steps up in front of me. And I'm looking at it now. Potential, Jake, it's there in you, but you gotta stop hiding from yourself. Wake up. Start wrestling with this life God gave you. Now come on, let's call the Bill.'

Sol reached out to help Jake, but it was Jake who helped Sol up and guided him out of the coal house. Jake wrenched the blade from his mutilated flesh and let out another flurry of swearing. Sol went into the house, found a couple of Cain's shirts and ripped them up for a tourniquet.

As they sat outside on the grass bank, the sun warming their faces, Sol shook his head in despair. 'I can't believe he killed Abby. Why would he do that?'

'Who knows . . . jealousy? Rage? Revenge for something? Were you in love with her?'

Sol laughed. 'What? Me? Love? No . . . I . . . me? Love her?'

The concept clearly pulled the rug from under him.

He shook his head repeatedly. 'I hardly knew her . . . I was just doing a favour for my old man. I mean . . . what's love anyway? I thought I knew once upon a time. I would like to have loved her. Believe me.' He frowned. 'I wrote a hell of a song about love once. Went on forever. The

"Bohemian Rhapsody" of romantic ballads. I wrote it for this girl. And she loved it. But I don't think she loved me. I think she liked the idea of loving me. Easy to fall in love with the idea of falling in love. That's much sweeter than the real thing if you ask me. Love's a hell of a word, mate. I guess I love Rhea. But I can't not love her . . .'

For a moment he was in another place, in an imaginary world, standing between his father and his wife.

'You don't love normal life,' she was saying, 'you have to love shopping and mess and diarrhoea and vomit and nits . . .'

'Dad,' Sol heard himself say. 'Why did you spend so much time with other people? I know you think I'm the dog's biscuit, but the point is you can't just say that. I'm right here. Stop the music and give me some time . . .'

Sol sighed and dragged his thoughts back. 'But maybe that's a different kind of love,' he said. 'When you've got a choice, it's harder. So much choice. Maybe I loved them all. All those women. Maybe it wasn't love at all . . . I can't believe he killed Abby. I really can't. She was so vibrant. So beautiful.'

He gazed at The Memphis across the road. Tamar was shaking doormats and drying off beer towels in the breeze. Just the sight of her brought back distracting memories for him.

They sat in silence for a while.

'When are those cops coming?' Jake muttered eventually and he adjusted the makeshift tourniquet. He needed to get to Casualty.

'I'm not sure what to do. I'm tempted to take off round the world. Maybe even twice. It's that or top myself.' Sol said it so easily, like he was ordering a pizza with extra cheese.

'I don't believe this. You just gave me a lecture about the evils of running away.'

The battle

Sol shrugged. 'We're all hypocrites,' he said. 'We'd all rather control other people and live our lives through them. It's easier than facing your own crap. Anyway, I'm not running, I'm exploring – I plan to come home again. I have to, I'm gonna take over the old man's business one day. And I have big plans for it.'

'How can you say that? How can you talk about topping yourself one minute, then say you got big plans for the future?'

Sol threw him a shrewd grin. 'The people who talk about suicide aren't the ones with a pocketful of pills and a spare hose for the exhaust.' Then he rubbed his head and added, 'It's just another option for those days when the meaning of life is nothing more than a dot on the horizon.'

Jake scowled and wound the rag tourniquet more tightly round his leg. 'My brother's gonna kill me,' he said. 'You see, for all your wise words, you got that bit wrong. Very wrong. Me kill him? You're kidding, mate. I can't kill him, I never could, he's too strong, he'll murder me.'

'I doubt it,' said Sol, pulling the hip flask from his pocket and passing it to Jake. 'Not with that leg. I guarantee that when he sees you limping over the horizon his heart will melt. His little brother, come home with a bad leg and a humble grin. He won't attack you, you're a wounded animal. Just make sure you can find a humble grin.'

'D'you think they'll catch Cain?' Jake gasped.

Sol shrugged. 'Who knows? But there is one thing I need to do, a promise I made.'

That cold blast of death

Cain was home, though it didn't feel like it any more. Back in the town where he grew up. Not far from the farm of his youth. He wandered about in a daze and found himself on the edge of a field that bordered the woods.

And suddenly he was back there. Walking in the open with her. It was a beautiful afternoon and the sun was going down. The place was deserted and there was nothing to disturb the peace. Nothing but the anger inside his heart and the murder lurking in his fingers.

She was holding her favourite DVD in her hands, wagging it at him as if he were a naughty schoolboy.
    'Shut up!' he was saying. 'Shut up!'
    She laughed. She always laughed at him.
    'Face it, Cain, it just wasn't good enough. You should try harder. I can't believe you took off like that. People thought it was a joke.'
    'Shut up!'
    'You never learn. You always think you can cut corners.'
    'I don't.'
    'You didn't even dress up.'
    'It was just some old royal guy. An old codger in a uniform.'

'It was important! A chance to do well. And you rolled up looking like the back shelf at Oxfam – they could see you were blagging it. I didn't need to say anything.'

She clicked her tongue and wagged the DVD again.

'Face it, big brother – you just weren't up to it – I'm not meaning to nag but you need to try harder, shape up! Some of us have it, some of us don't . . .'

She was joking but he couldn't see it. There was too much red mist clouding his vision. Too much sin crouching at his door.

And that's when he led her away from the field, beyond the trees and into a clearing just big enough to grab her by the neck, hurl her to the ground and tear the life from her. She fought back for a while, and her fist pummelled the back of his hand as he gripped her neck. Her nails dug deep and drew blood but he wasn't deterred: he held on and squeezed and twisted. Then he stood back and kicked again and again and again. Until there was no more screaming and fighting from her. Just the blood, pooling around her beautiful head and her soft blonde hair. So much blood, so much beauty, mixed there in the dirt. And silence. Ghostly, menacing silence. Her green and blue eyes frozen and fixed, staring ahead. And nearby her favourite film lying in the dirt, a little dam blocking the course of the stream of blood that leaked away from her. He never meant to kill her, he just wanted to teach her a lesson, but the lesson went on and on, until there was nothing left of her to teach.

And now he was back there, really back there, standing in the field, peeking through the gap in the trees that led to that little killing ground. He could feel his head swim and his palms sweat. The sensation was overwhelming.

And she was there too. Abby standing there with blood seeping from the huge gashes in her face. 'Why've you come back?' she whispered, her voice dry and weak. 'To do me more damage?'

'I can't do you more damage.'

'No, but you can't repair me either, you can't bring me back, Cain. You should never have done it. See that mark – that stain on your hand. That'll always remind you. You're flawed, Cain. Your soul has a fracture running through it.'

He grimaced. 'It's not fair.'

'Yes, it is. You knew what you were doing. You gave in to the dark side.'

'Grief! . . . you make it sound like this is *Star Wars*.'

Abby's black eyes widened. There was heavy swelling around the sockets.

'You had a choice. You should have fought it. You didn't have to do what you did. Evil was hanging around you like a bad smell. You didn't have to go with it; you could have fought it off. We all have choices, Cain. You never even started to fight. You just gave in.'

'It had been coming a long time,' he said. 'The hatred festered – it grew like fungus. You nurtured it. You made my life misery.'

'No, I didn't, you did – you just gave into envy and greed. Life is hard, Cain, hard! On this planet you have trouble. Everyone does. That's the way. You have to live with it and adjust.'

'It was too hard – you stole every good chance I ever got. Every chance. You couldn't leave me alone. Don't lecture me now about doing the right thing.'

'I loved you, you were my cosy big brother. What happened to you?'

He went silent for a moment, then he spat out the answer. 'You happened, Abby, you happened. I was fine till you came along and stole my dad. The moment you appeared I was doomed, you took every spare moment, every ounce of strength he had. We were fine till you showed up.'

He fell silent again, as if reconsidering, then he forced a smile. 'At least it's good to see you again,' he said.

She stared at him, her face deathly white, her eyes flickering like a neon sign.

'Don't kid yourself, Cain,' she said. 'You'll never stop seeing me now. Wherever you go I'll be on your shoulder, that cold blast of gentle death lurking behind you, waiting to chill the blood in your veins once and for all. Watch yourself big brother, 'cause one day you'll be me, one day you'll be no more . . .'

Cain glanced down at the mark on the back of his hand.

'That's why you have that, you'll always have that now. It'll be there to remind you of where you're headed. It'll mark you out as different. Fear and respect. It'll bring you both. And loneliness.'

'It's not fair, it's too much. My life'll be hell.'

'You'll survive. Though at times you might wish you hadn't . . .'

Before he knew it he was lunging for her, hands ready to choke the last vestige of life from her grey throat, fists poised to pummel her weak body all over again. But of course there was nothing to grab. She sidestepped his grasp easily.

'You see Cain – you're at it again. What's changed? What have you learned?'

She shook her head, turned and walked between the trees, melting into the foliage as she went.

Cain stood watching for a long time, willing her to come back, not only to him, but to life too. It wasn't going to happen. He stayed there until the dark fell and his bones were like chilled lead. Then he limped, stiff-legged and frozen, into a nearby Starbucks. He sat at a distant table, in a darkened area roped off for cleaning, nursing an Americano, and considering his options. He laid a strip of white sugar on the table. He could find the nearest police station and just give himself up, though a life behind bars might kill him. He laid a strip of brown sugar next to the white. He could return to Peniel Green and Renegade's Rest. Seek solace with Tamar and hope that she wouldn't sell him out. He might even find some kind of future with her, two broken people slotting the twisted fragments of their lives together. He laid a strip of sugar substitute next to the other two. Or he could just keep running. Spend the rest of his life on the move. Never come to a peaceful place, never stop glancing over his shoulder, always in fear of bumping into Sol or Jake, or worse still, his old man, Adam.

He looked at the three strips. Rearranged them, made shapes with them, tried every which way to make them look appealing. He failed. In the end he scooped up all three, downed the dregs of the Americano and limped out of Starbucks into the dark night.

Nod's Car Hire

Cain walked into the car hire place the next day, a smile a mile wide stretched across his face. He looked for all the world as if he'd been born again – a new man for a new day. No one would have guessed he'd spent the night walking across fields to get to that town. Two hours' sleep in an old barn and a quick wash in some public toilets and he was ready for action.

He chatted a lot to the assistant, gave his full name and details, date of birth, half his life history. As much as was necessary, he didn't spare details.

Then he flashed a final smile, scooped up the keys and drove the hire car away. Right away. Miles and miles, until the tank was nearly empty and the coast came into sight. Then he lined up the vehicle so it was square onto the cliff edge. The drop below was big enough. He threw as many clothes as he could spare inside. Then he took a deep breath, steeled himself, and the car plummeted over the edge. The end of everything. No more Cain. No more wandering. He stood on the cliff and watched his phantom self crash into the sea below. There'd be no body of course, but the sea was wild enough to suggest they'd never find one anyway. And if nothing else it gave him time to move on and start again. Another man in another place. Another chance. Perhaps he'd move to the middle of nowhere. Start his own community. Build his own little city where his past was a blank page.

Somewhere with bigger walls against the outside world, more corners to hide in. He'd tried living in the world and it was no ball game. He'd had enough of that. He'd find a place where other people couldn't touch him. A new life where he could avoid life. Carve out a niche just big enough for himself. A place to bide his time until there was no more time. He shivered and realised he needed more clothes. That meant getting a credit card. Somehow, somewhere, he'd find one he could *borrow*. The past was already catching him up again.

In a nearby town he found what he was looking for: a carelessly placed bag, tossed down by a bench on the railway station. It didn't take him long to free the purse from it and ease his way casually back out of the station. The moment he left, he spotted the other thing he was looking for, right across from the station entrance: a tattoo parlour.

The grieving unit

Sol hovered at the broken gate to the allotments. Two figures were working together on the land. It looked like hard going. Sol stood watching them for a while. They must have once made a good-looking couple. He leant on the bar and it gave off a loud crack. Adam looked up. Eve was standing with him; they looked desperately small in that large field. Sol sighed and forced a smile. This was not going to be easy. He felt a hand on his shoulder. It was Seth, he was standing just behind him. Seth smiled.

'Abby's not coming back, is she?'

Sol shook his head. 'Never,' he said, 'and neither is Cain. I don't know how to tell them.'

'It's not your job,' said Seth. 'Thanks for coming. I'll do it. I'll look after them now.'

Sol turned and started to walk away, but he couldn't go, something held him back. He felt like a street kid spying on the rich people; he couldn't stop himself. He leant against a tree and watched from the leafy shadows. Seth went straight to his parents and they moved in close to him to listen. Eve gasped and fell against him; Seth steadied her and pulled her to himself. Adam let out something between a shout and a groan; there was anger and regret in his voice. The three of them fell into each other and began to cry. The little reduced family sobbed loudly and uncontrollably, like a single grieving unit. Sol had never seen anything like it before in his life. In a strange way, he envied Seth.

Home

Jake pulled the car over and parked it in a lay-by. Far enough away from home to be hidden. He clambered out and winced as he put strain on his wounded leg. The dressing felt secure enough, but the doctor had warned him to keep his weight off it for a while.

'Don't go running any marathons!'

Or limping the last half mile home. But he was taking Sol's advice, not the doc's. He needed to face his brother and he needed to win his sympathy. It wasn't a scam. Jake was wounded, broken on the inside too. He just required an opportunity to show Esau that was the case. He'd picked a time when he figured they'd be home. Eating together. The wide-screen television news belching at them from the corner of the room. He hadn't even wanted his mother to know he was coming.

He'd wondered about sending something: flowers or chocolates or a hamper. He'd drifted around the city shops for a while, absorbed in the shelves piled high with potential presents. He'd carried a stack of music and DVDs to the till at one point, but then he'd put them all back. No point trying to seduce them with treasure. He was bringing news of new life: that was enough, surely. He sincerely hoped so. It was all he really had himself. He locked the car and started walking. The old house was set back from the road: he'd have to limp up the long gravelled drive to get anywhere near the front door.

A figure was standing in the parking bay in front of the building. Staring off into the distance. Was it his brother? Jake hadn't eaten for a while but he felt like he was about to cough up the last three days of food. He stood there, between the double gates, his breath coming in short gasps, the blood pumping in his temples. The scrapes on his face pounded as his heartbeat speeded up.

He thought he could hear that familiar rasping voice. 'I told you I'd find you. Say your prayers, brother, 'cause they're long overdue.'

'Esau?' Jake mouthed the question silently, but the figure was too far away to hear or be heard. The voices played in his head.

He had to force himself to take one step at a time: his shoes felt as if they were full of concrete, every step tore at the ligaments in his legs. He was never going to make it down the drive. The shadowy figure in the drive turned and stared at him. It paused, then took a step closer, a step towards him. If it was Esau, then he was bigger than Jake remembered.

Way bigger.

Jake forced himself to keep walking. He hated every inch of the journey, every fibre in his being was yelling at him to turn and flee. But he limped on, inch after inch, one leaden footstep at a time.

'It's you, isn't it?' Jake said, still too quietly to be heard.

The figure started to move towards him down the drive, one fist gripped inside the other. Gravel crunched and stray twigs snapped as they walked on towards each other. Twigs or the sound of his brother's knuckles cracking . . .

Another couple of steps from the dark figure. He was growing taller by the second. Jake began to regret the lack of chocolates and flowers and reconciliatory presents.

'Look, I've got money, lots of it, you can have it all. Look – I've got a beautiful old church – it's worth a fortune. Take that too. You can have anything – everything. It's all yours . . .' The voice in his head screamed on.

Esau could kill him with his bare hands. Jake knew that. He did kick boxing and played American football. Jake did crosswords and played records. No one could call that an even match. The figure took another step and Jake looked around to run, but it was too late; he should have chosen that option twenty seconds ago. Anywhere he ran now, he'd be within tackling distance of his brother. Running wasn't an option anyway: with this leg he'd just crumble to the ground like a wounded animal.

The figure stepped into the evening light and Jake got the shock of his life. It wasn't Esau: it was his dad. It was dear old Isaac, frail like himself, walking and limping and leaning on a stick. His eyes had played tricks; the figure wasn't a giant at all.

'Dad . . .' Jake's throat was dry, his lips felt like cardboard.

'Who's that . . . ? Jake . . . ?' The old man swung his head round in Jake's direction, his blind eyes flicking right and left in their sockets.

'Yeah, Dad, it's me . . .'

The old man fell towards him and wrapped his arms around Jake.

Jake half expected the meeting to turn into another fight, another bad dream. But there were no threats or shouting. Instead Isaac began to sob. Long and hard. His body slammed repeatedly into Jake as he gasped for every breath. Eventually, as the tears subsided, Isaac stood back and pressed his hands against the face of his lost boy.

'I missed you so much, son, I missed you. I really did. Every day I looked for you, came limping down this drive, every day I was ready to take you back. You didn't need to stay away.'

'But I took everything you had, Dad, all that money you'd saved for years, I blew it all . . .'

'Shut up,' Isaac said, and he shoved tears from his eyes with the back of his hand. 'Let's waste some more money and have a party.'

'What's going on?'

It was Esau. His father stepped to one side and there he was. His huge brother, beer bottle in one hand and carving knife in the other.

'It's Jake,' Isaac spluttered, 'Look! He's back. He's back! How many days have we prayed for this?'

There was movement behind Esau and Rebekah appeared in the doorway, her red hair blazing behind her as she ran. She threw herself at Jake and knocked him off his feet. They fell to the ground together and he could hear her laughing and screaming and crying.

'What's wrong with your leg?' Esau said, his face solid and staring. 'You got injured.'

He pointed at Jake's thigh with the carving knife.

'I'm OK,' Jake said, hauling himself from the ground, but as he said it, his thigh spasmed and he fell heavily, gravel digging into his knees.

'Argh!'

He felt a hand on his arm and a shoulder taking his weight and lifting him up. He smelt beer and turned and saw his brother holding him effortlessly.

'Let's get you inside,' he said. 'We got plenty to talk about.'

'You're gonna be an uncle,' Jake muttered, as they supported him through the door, 'might even be twins.'

'Really? You've been busy.' And for the first time Esau produced a smile.

The favour

Jake woke up the next morning and immediately felt for all four limbs. He couldn't believe it. Apart from the wound in his left leg, everything was intact. Yet here he was in his old bed, in his old room, in his old home. He lay motionless for a while, piecing the story back together in his head. Then he laughed. He couldn't quite believe it was all true. He'd made it back home and he was still alive. All those nightmares, all that stress and anguish. It had come to nothing. He was back and it was all going to be OK.

Then he heard the shouting. Esau's unmistakable bark seeping through the house from the kitchen. He got up slowly, took the stick his old man had given him and limped gingerly through the house.

Esau was in the kitchen with his dad. Jake hovered by the doorway, just out of sight.

'But he owes!' Esau was blathering. 'He owes! He owes! You, Mum, me. Especially me! That was my inheritance. My money. It's one thing to welcome him back with open arms . . .'

'Face it Esau, we thought he was dead. We thought he was gone for ever.'

'Yeah, and good riddance. At least that solved the problem of retribution. Now that he's back the wound's open again. He must pay his debts. It's not fair. It's just not . . . oh, hello Jake.'

Jake showed his face and came limping into the kitchen. Isaac looked embarrassed. He looked so much frailer than Jake remembered; the stroke had taken its toll. His breathing was strained too, his breath came in shallow rasping blasts from his chest. He leant against the kitchen surface. Jake couldn't resist going over and putting a hand on him. This wasn't the old man he'd come to resent, this was the failing father who needed his sons.

'I'll pay,' Jake whispered.

'You can't,' said Isaac. 'It's too much.'

'I have property,' Jake said.

'You'll need it,' said Isaac, 'you're going to have a family.'

'We'll find somewhere smaller.'

'Too right you will,' Esau blundered on. 'I want every penny back.'

It seemed as if a night's sleep had restored his brother's old-fashioned sense of justice.

'Easy – shut up,' said Isaac. 'In this family there's been enough animosity. Let's dig a little deeper and find some forgiveness.'

'He is forgiven. You know that. Grief! If he wasn't he'd be lying there in a pool of his own blood. I'm letting him off lightly.'

'Then you're not letting him off at all.'

'Grief, Dad! You've changed your tune. Think about this. Think about your fortune. Think how easily it slipped out of the door in his back pocket. Think how easily he played the part of me and made an idiot out of you.'

Isaac slapped his hand down on the kitchen surface beside him. The sound echoed in the house. 'I have thought! You know I have. Night after night after night. I've not been negligent about that. I've thought on it so

The favour

faithfully that it gave me this.' He tapped his fist against his temple. 'I've nurtured vengeful ambitions so much it corroded my brain and corrupted my body.' He jammed the end of his stick into Esau's shoulder. 'Now I think I've done enough thinking on it. I'm getting a taste for grace and believe me – it's a hell of a lot more palatable.'

'Then you're getting weak,' Esau muttered.

Isaac slammed his hand again. 'No, Esau – you're the weak one. Forgiving Jake is not a cop-out, believe me. And you will see it for what it is. There'll be no retribution. No punishment. No payment.'

Esau's mouth fell open. 'But think about it, Dad. That's naïve. He'll just do it again. You can't let him off lightly. It's in his nature.'

There was silence in the kitchen. A soft footfall sounded in the doorway and Rebekah entered. 'Jake's changed. Clearly, Esau – you haven't,' she said, and it sounded so final that no one said any more. She gave a huge smile. 'Now who wants eggs?'

A phone rang. They looked for their mobiles; Esau seething and muttering as he searched. In the end it turned out to be Jake's. He took the call outside on the drive.

'Hello?'

'Hey mate – you're still alive then? They haven't beaten you to a pulp? See, I told you all you needed was that limp and a humble grin.'

It was Sol.

'Where are you?' Jake asked. He could hear the sound of a tannoy in the background and voices echoing on a busy concourse.

'Nearly in paradise, mate, nearly in paradise. Just wanted to send you on a wild goose chase.'

'What?'

'Well, more of a treasure hunt. It'll be worth your while mate. Got internet access out in the sticks there?'

'Sure, why?'

'Take these numbers. 492 781, 555 2 907 7. Got 'em?'

'Yeah, but why?'

'Enjoy, mate. I'm off to Graceland. One of many stops on my world tour. I'll get a T-shirt printed and send you one. Give my love to your brother.'

And the line went dead.

Back in the kitchen the air was thick with tension and the smell of cooking eggs.

'Who was that?' his mother asked, trying her best to sound breezy.

'My friend Sol.'

'What – that rich kid who was always getting off with the girls?' said Esau. 'He was a right loser.'

'I don't think so,' said Jake. 'What does this number look like to you?'

They crowded round Jake to see the scribble on the back of his hand.

'A combination?'

'Phone number? Deposit box?'

Jake dialled the number. Nothing. It didn't register and the line died. He tried again, but it was the same result.

'Could be a safe combination,' said Jake.

'Why? You trying to run off with someone else's money?'

'Easy!' Isaac snapped and he cracked his older son across the shoulders with his stick.

Esau shrugged. 'Just asking.'

'It's a bank account,' said Rebekah. 'Look – 49 27 81 – that's a sort code.'

'I need the internet,' Jake said.

He googled the sort code and sure enough, after a convoluted search, a branch in London showed up.

He went out into the huge back garden; there was drizzle in the morning air. Jake stood on the perfectly manicured oval lawn surrounded by finely tuned hedges. All Esau's work. He dialled the phone number. The others watched through the kitchen window. He tried to forget about them. His father looking weak and curious, his mother shrewd and hopeful, his brother still seething and wrestling with his instinct for revenge. He put them out of his mind. A robin perched in the hedge, it flew down and chirped cheerily by his foot. It wasn't afraid.

A telephonist took the call and passed him on. 'Mr Canaan? Mr Jake Canaan? Can you give me your date of birth please?'

He did.

'Mother's maiden name? Place of birth? That's great. What was the account number again?'

Jake repeated it.

'Yes, I can verify that is an account we hold. It's registered in your name and has recently received a payment. A considerable payment. Would you like to know the exact amount?'

You bet Jake would.

He listened and nodded and the truth hit him. Somehow Sol had opened an account in his name. He asked one more question.

'The only details we can supply are those attached to the payment. Just a simple phrase, I'm afraid. It reads, *A favour for a favour*. Will that be all? Thanks very much for your business today. If we can advise you regarding the balance of this account, please let us know. A deposit of this size has a lot of possibilities.'

Jake hung up and closed the phone. He went back inside.

'I don't get it,' he said, shaking his head, 'he didn't owe me a favour. He owes me nothing.'

'What is it? Was it an account?' his mother asked.

Jake nodded. He glanced at his brother and gave him a sheepish grin.

'You needn't worry about your money, Esau. It's all sorted.'

He dialed Sol's number.

'The Orange mobile you are calling is currently switched off. You may leave a message after the . . .'

He hung up. 'I can't believe it,' he said. 'He really doesn't owe me this.'

PART FIVE

The Good Lover's Sex Guide

'Ugh!'

Reuben threw down the paperback with a disgusted growl. It bounced off the carriage seat and landed on the floor, denting the spine as it did so. Jake bent down and scooped it up.

'That's weird!' said Reuben.

'Easy,' said Jake, 'that's by an old friend of mine. And you shouldn't be reading it anyway.'

Waterstone's was packed. It was only to be expected. *The Good Lover's Sex Guide* was falling off the shelves, it was so popular. And with the author in to do a signing, it was doing even better.

'Do I get royalties?'

Sol glanced up, his pen poised over the latest copy. He was about to scribble his usual comment *Make love and keep us all happy*, then he saw her, standing right in front of him. It had been a while. Tamar had aged a little; he guessed her hair had help to stay so black these days. But in general she was wearing well and looking good.

'Well, you know what I mean – I see I'm in it,' she said. 'Goodness. Is that a blush in your cheeks, Sol King?'

'What are you doing here?' he rasped, his throat unexpectedly dry.

'What do you think? I came to get my book signed. It's very entertaining, by the way. So, do I?'

'Do you what?'

'Get royalties.'

Sol squirmed a little.

'And look who else has bought a copy as well,' she said. She gestured towards the huge mountain of books stacked majestically like some sort of regal temple by the door. Dinah looked over and gave him a wink.

'And surprise surprise – look who's with her,' said Tamar.

Dinah jabbed her thumb over her shoulder and a familiar-looking woman gave him a cheesy grin, then waved. Sol frowned.

'I never could remember her name,' he said quietly to Tamar.

'I know, and so does she. They're both in here though, aren't they?' she tapped the book. 'We all are.'

'It's, er . . . based on many experiences.'

'I'll bet. Did you have fun writing it?'

Sol sighed, took a book from a nearby punter and scribbled his signature across the flyleaf. He gave the guy a quick smile then looked back at Tamar.

'I wrote most of it a long time ago. On a train journey ten years back.'

'Ten years. Hmm. Interesting. That would make sense, that was about the time we were all . . . making . . . er, *hay* . . . together. Quite a productive period, then.'

She was enjoying every minute of this.

'What do you want?' Sol said. 'Money?'

Tamar looked genuinely offended.

'Sol, you know me better than that, I'm not some cash-grabbing tart, you know. To be honest, we heard you were here and thought we'd make your day.'

Sol allowed himself a smile. 'Well . . . you've made it memorable,' he said, and he took her book and scribbled in it.

'So? Did you settle down then?' she asked.

Sol paused. 'Not really. You?'

She shook her head. 'Not really.'

They looked at each other for a long time. People came and went, Sol glanced away occasionally and signed a few books, but it felt as if everything was moving in slow motion.

'I guess some people just never do,' she said eventually, her eyes still locked on his, and he nodded.

'Dad, check these.' A pretty teenager with green and purple hair and a line of studs across her right eyebrow called across to Sol. She came over and showed him a couple of books. Sol took them and laughed.

'You have to get these for your mother,' he said.

'Is this . . .' Tamar frowned. 'No! It can't be. Rhea?'

The girl nodded.

'I was a good friend of your mum's,' Tamar said, 'but it must be five or six years since I saw you.'

'I went off to boarding school ages ago,' the girl said.

'Is it OK? Are you OK?'

'Yeah. My dad's a sex guru. My mates all love it.'

And she slipped off again, teaming up with a punk in a tartan kilt and a Slits T-shirt on the other side of the shop.

'Time moves on, Tamar,' Sol said. 'The world turns and life goes around and comes around.'

'Yeah, yeah, save your philosophy for your next book,' she said.

'That is from my next book. Thought I might call it Ecclesiastes.'

'What's that mean?'

Sol shrugged. 'The philosophy of life.'

'Good luck with that,' she said with a wry smile.

'D'you still have The Memphis?'

'Yeah, Peniel Green is quieter than ever these days, I feel like I'm on a desert island sometimes. You should come round. Or is the place too insignificant for a famous dude like you now?'

Sol smiled and pulled a jet-black card from his pocket. 'Call me,' he said, handing it to her.

But she shook her head and slipped it back on the table. 'Call me,' she said, 'I'm in the phone book.'

She kissed her index finger and pressed it on the card.

'Be seeing you, stud,' she said and she hooked up with Dinah and the other girl and was gone.

Sol was still staring after them when his phone rang a minute later.

'Hello? Sol King.'

'Hi Sol, my son hates your book. He says it's strange and embarrassing.'

'Jake! How you doing?'

'I'm OK.'

'Which son is this?'

'Oh, Reuben, and his opinion ain't to be trifled with. Mind you, he's only ten and he thought it was the good socks guide. He prefers science fiction. He's here now, we're on our way to his mum's. I hope it was OK to call you? I got your number from your PA – things have been going well for you.'

'Yeah, I'm running the studio now. Dad just sits in the background, strumming his guitar and talking about the old days.'

'I read about your new label.'

'Oh yeah, Song of Songs, it's gonna be massive, man, we're turning out some sexy tunes right now. Five in the top ten downloads.'

'You sound like your dad, mate.'

'Yeah, I'm turning into him, I think. What about you? Still on Sunshine Radio?'

'No, I went up a level, chat show on Sky. I miss the music though, I think it's what they call the Peter Principal – got offered more money for doing what I don't do best. That was another reason for calling, d'you wanna come on and do an interview about the book? A, er . . . favour for a favour?'

Sol laughed. 'Why? What you offering in return?'

'First up the chance to advertise your new book, and second a meal with me and the missus and the tribe.'

'You still in that draughty old castle?'

'It's a chapel.'

'How's Leah's cooking these days?'

'Not bad, but Rach's is better.'

'What?'

There was a short silence on the other end of the line. Jake said something to his son and then spoke again in muttered tones. 'Hang on, just going for a walk.' Then a minute later, 'Me and Leah went separate ways, I married Rach, she's pregnant with my seventh.'

'Seventh?'

'Well, I already had six with Leah, she loves kids. It's great news for Rach though, she thought she couldn't have any.'

'You have *six* kids? Jake – you were about to slash your wrists over one.'

'I know, life's messy, eh? I think a great man told me that once. Just as he was about to jam a chisel into my leg. Thanks by the way, I feel I never said a proper thank you.'

'For the chisel?'

'No, you know what I mean. The money.'

'Oh man, it was nothing, I hardly noticed it leave my account. I'm filthy rich, don't you know.'

'You saved my life, Sol.'

'Well, in an odd kind of way you saved mine.'

There was an embarrassed silence at both ends of the line. Then Jake cleared his throat.

'I never got a chance to ask you about the world tour. How was it?'

'Yeah, it was cool. Stumbled across a lot of new music along the way, smuggled most of it back with me too.'

'Did you find yourself?'

Sol laughed. 'I still came back wondering if it's all meaningless really. I'm with Bono – still haven't found what I'm looking for. Hey – I hear good things of Leah.'

'Yup, she's just a cut a new album, her fourth I think. Twenty soul classics.'

'That'll sell well, especially with her sound. I never understand why she's not broken into the big time. I'd be happy to work with her . . .'

'Ah, she does all right. She's worked out what she wants and she's making a living doing it. She's happy.'

'What? Even with you shacked up with her sister?'

'Pass. Let's just say she wasn't queuing up to sing "I will survive" at the wedding.'

'I bet her old man was well chuffed about it all!'

'To be honest, I think he was bewildered by the whole thing. Six kids by one sister, then I go and marry the other one. He hasn't offered me a job in the company. The office parties would have been awkward. He's glad Rach is safe back from her travels in Asia though.'

'What?'

'Never mind,' said Jake, 'long story. Actually Laban's business is in trouble these days: he's not done so well lately. Rach says it's my fault – his business was booming till I started messing with his family.'

Sol paused and signed a clutch of books from a posse of embarrassed teenagers. Jake waited then went on. 'So,' he said, 'what do you say to my offer? Will you come over and flirt with my wife? She does a mean biryani.'

'Maybe. What channel's your show go out on?'

'Sky Showbiz . . . four.'

'Four! No way, that gets an audience of three and one of them's a dog. I'll think about it . . .'

Sol froze. The figure in front of him was chillingly familiar.

The hand resting on the open book in front of him bore a large black tattoo.

'What the?'

'What's wrong?' he heard Jake ask down the phone.

'I think someone just walked over my grave.'

His face was a little more lined and the Mohawk had been replaced by short brown stubble, greying at the temples. He wore a swaggering *I'm in charge* kind of suit, but underneath it there was still the same lanky bean-pole frame.

'You got a nerve,' Sol said quietly, glancing around the shop. Everyone was carrying on as if there were nothing unusual happening.

'Don't bother calling the cops,' Cain said. 'I'll be long gone before they even put their doughnuts down.' His voice had a menacing purr to it, as if he was used to manipulating his listeners.

'So they never found you, eh?'

'And they won't. But I couldn't resist dropping by when I saw you were on a book tour. Is it then? A *good* sex guide?'

'Why did you do it?'

'What?' Cain's pale features creased into a frown. His eyes remained cold and distant. His emotions were locked away somewhere in a hermetically sealed box.

'I've always wanted to ask you – why did you kill her?'

'I don't know what you're talking about, Mr King, and if you were as streetwise as they claim, you'd know not to ask that. Autograph, please.'

Sol looked at the book in Cain's hand. 'Go to hell.'

'Oh, I have been, and back. But I've put it all behind me now. I run my own little community, you know. A sort of place of refuge. A place of rehabilitation for those that . . . struggle to fit in. Those that find themselves on the wrong side of justice, a place the rebels can call home. It's an efficient operation, a kind of self-sufficient community farm. You'd be impressed. It's a place for people like us.'

'Us? Don't even begin down that road. You and I are poles apart.'

'Not really. We've both been disappointed and confused by the outcome of life. You make a living out of it, I have built a place of refuge. A place with thick walls so people can rant and rave and protect themselves from the world.'

'Sounds like purgatory.'

'I made a home for myself. And others like me. A place for the restless, for those . . . misunderstood by society.'

Sol gestured at the black tattoo. 'I see you still have the mark,' he said.

For the first time Cain faltered. He glanced around but no one was taking any notice.

'Apparently it'll always be there. So I figured I might as well decorate it. Make a feature of it.'

'Hide it, you mean.'

Cain gave a reptilian smile and tapped the mark on his hand. 'You know where that came from?'

Sol shook his head. 'I don't care,' he said.

'Oh, I think you do. It's a reminder. When I . . . was last with my sister, after all that took place . . . this mark appeared . . . I couldn't get rid of it. Nothing would take it off. It's always seemed like a mark of retribution. A mark of hopelessness and wandering. Well, I found a way to transform it. And now I live with it.'

'In your own little self-obsessed world.'
'You should come and visit some time.'
'Oh I'd love to, just give me the address . . .'
Another reptilian smile.

'No. On second thoughts, I'd better not. No autograph then?' Cain offered the book.

Sol stared at it.

'Sol? Sol? What's going on?' Sol had forgotten the phone. Jake was still waiting.

'Don't I deserve an epitaph? I came a long way to see you,' Cain said.

'You know who's on the other end of here?' Sol held up the phone.

'Not the other one? Not the blond guy? Oh, this is sweet. Both of you in one hit.'

And before Sol could stop him Cain reached down and picked up the mobile in his tattooed hand.

'Mr Canaan, I hear you're a family man now?'

'What? Sol? Who's this?'

'I haven't a lot of time for the likes of you but here's something you can reflect on into your old age. If you ever, ever come looking for me, and it'll be a thankless task, just remember that I've done my homework and I know all about you, where you live, what you do, and who you love. I have friends and you have a family to protect. Goodbye Jake, I don't expect to ever see you again.' And he handed the phone back to Sol.

'That kind of wraps it up,' Cain said. 'Still no autograph? Well, I tried, maybe when my life story comes out you'll regret treating me so bitterly. Nice to see you again, Sol, look after that pretty daughter of yours.'

And he was gone. Sol watched for a moment then he was up, he couldn't help himself, he was in the shop doorway, gaping up and down the street, his head flicking from side to side.

'Sol? What the hell was that all about?'

Sol put the phone to his ear. 'It was Cain, mate. He's alive. He was here.'

Jake gasped. 'Oh my . . .'

'Oops! Oh! Hi, remember me?' The figure coming into the shop was moving so swiftly the two men collided. Sol took a step back and eyed the smiling face. For a moment he thought Cain was back.

'Seth?'

'Well remembered. We only met, what? Twice?'

'Yeah, but I'll never forget that second time.'

'You were kind, it was really good of you to come back. You could have just left it to the police . . .'

'Come in, come in, what you doing here?'

'What d'you think? I've come to get my signed copy. Actually I was hoping you'd remember me and I wanted to brag about knowing someone famous.'

They went in. Seth hadn't changed much. It looked as if good living had served him well.

'Jake, don't go, I'll be back,' Sol said into his phone.

'We're nearly at the station, Sol, and this is costing me a fortune. And Reuben wants to call Billy.'

'Who's Billy?'

'His girlfriend.'

'Girlfriend? He's started young, he's ten.'

'Yeah, well, you'd know about that.'

'Wait. I'll be back.'

Before Jake could hang up, he lowered the phone and sat down on the table next to his books. 'Here, Seth, have a free copy,' Sol scribbled on a book and handed it over.

Seth looked embarrassed. 'Gosh, well, if you're sure . . .'

'I'm sure. Hey, I don't suppose you . . . well, d'you ever wonder about Cain?'

The smile left Seth's face.

'What is there to wonder? We put it behind us. He's gone, didn't you see the stories about the car accident?'

'Oh yeah, sure, the car accident. So how's your mum and dad?'

Seth smiled again. 'Yep, they're OK, we turned the business around, converted some of the old buildings into holiday lets, and farmed out some of the land. My wife and I run the business. She's pregnant now, so things look good. Why do you ask about Cain?'

Sol studied the younger guy's face. The years had not taken their toll: the optimism still lurked in those eyes.

'No reason,' he said. 'Like you say, it's all gone now. The past is the past.'

Seth looked perplexed but he just nodded. 'Hey,' he said, 'do they have anything on women giving birth?'

'It's Waterstone's – they have everything. They probably have something on men giving birth.'

Seth went looking.

Sol raised his phone. 'Jake? Listen, I'd better go, mate.'

'What? You kept me waiting to tell me that? Reuben's going spare here.'

'I just wanted to tell you I'll do your show. It'll be a pleasure, mate. Maybe I'll bring Rhea too. She's started writing a few songs these days.'

'Brilliant. Thanks, mate. I'll call you to fix a time. It's been too long, we should stay in touch.'

Final breaths

By the time Jake drew his last breath he had twelve sons and one daughter. Rach tragically died after complications giving birth to their youngest child, Ben. The baby was healthy and came through it all right, but Jake pined for Rach for the rest of his life. Some time after this, Leah (who had never stopped loving him) and Jake moved in together again. They had so many children in common it seemed ridiculous not to do so. Jake put his heart and soul into the marriage and they stayed together, though he never stopped loving Rach. His children turned out to be a diverse and creative bunch who did various ill-advised things and were often at odds – but none ever attempted to cheat their old man out of inheritance money. Over the years Jake did well in broadcasting, through good times and bad. He eventually retired and left Bethel Chapel to Reuben. He had had two sons by Rach: Ben and Joe. Joe was a brilliant administrator and the apple of his dad's eye: he eventually became Managing Director of Sky Broadcasting.

Sol ran the Song of Songs label for forty years, and made Radio Therapy one of the most powerful studios in the world. When he died, he'd still not settled down with one woman, and had produced fifteen kids from various relationships. Rhea took on the business after him and ran it for a further seventeen years. After that, various family feuds broke out which split the music dynasty. There were lawsuits and very public wranglings over money and it was never the same again. Sol and Tamar remained friends and he often visited her at The Memphis, thought he never got used to the dogs. Then one night the place was gutted by a huge fire while he was staying over. He helped rescue Tamar and subsequently financed a new pub for her, the Absalom.

Throughout his life Sol kept searching hard but never really found what he was looking for, though ironically he did enable a lot of others to crack that problem.

And Cain? Who knows where he ended his days? Or if he found peace? Sol never saw him again after that day in Waterstone's, and as far as is known, he never served time for murdering his sister Abby.